ANNOUNCING THE HAVERGAL EDITION
NOW IN PREPARATION FOR PUBLICATION

The edition of *The Complete Works of Frances Ridley Havergal* has five parts:

Volume I *Behold Your King:*
The Complete Poetical Works of Frances Ridley Havergal

Volume II *Whose I Am and Whom I Serve:*
Prose Works of Frances Ridley Havergal

Volume III *Loving Messages for the Little Ones:*
Works for Children by Frances Ridley Havergal

Volume IV *Love for Love: Frances Ridley Havergal:*
Memorials, Letters and Biographical Works

Volume V *Songs of Truth and Love:*
Music by Frances Ridley Havergal and William Henry Havergal

David L. Chalkley, Editor   Dr. Glen T. Wegge, Music Editor

The Music of Frances Ridley Havergal by Glen T. Wegge, Ph.D.

This Companion Volume to the Havergal edition is a valuable presentation of
F.R.H.'s extant scores. Except for a very few of her hymn scores published in hymn-
books, most or nearly all of F.R.H.'s scores have been very little—if any at all—seen,
or even known of, for nearly a century. What a valuable body of music has been unknown for so long and is now made available to many. Dr. Wegge completed his
Ph.D. in Music Theory at Indiana University at Bloomington, and his diligence and
thoroughness in this volume are obvious. First an analysis of F.R.H.'s compositions
is given, an essay that both addresses the most advanced musicians and also reaches those who are untrained in music; then all the extant scores that have been found
are newly typeset, with complete texts for each score and extensive indices at the end
of the book. This volume presents F.R.H.'s music in newly typeset scores diligently
prepared by Dr. Wegge, and Volume V of the Havergal edition presents the scores
in facsimile, the original 19th century scores. (The essay—a dissertation—analysing
her scores is given the same both in this Companion Volume and in Volume V of
the Havergal edition.)

Dr. Wegge is also preparing all of these scores for publication in performance fo-
lio editions.

Jn. 3. 8.
Ps. 45. 1.
Jo 20. 18, 25.
CHAPTER I.

v. 4. 20.
c. 40. 4.
THAT which was from the *a* beginning, which we have heard, which we have seen *c* with our eyes, which we have looked upon, and our hands have *d* handled, of the Word of life;

2 (For the life was manifested, and we have seen *it*, and bear witness, and shew unto you that eternal life, *f* which was with the Father, and was manifested unto us;)

He. 4. 20.
1 Ju. 2. 7.
Ju. 10. 32.
3 That which we have seen and heard declare we unto you, that ye also may have fellowship with us: and truly our fellowship *l* is with the Father, and with

Co. 1. 9.
his Son Jesus Christ.

4 And these things write we unto you, that *n* your joy may be full.

1 c. v. 5-7
5 This then is the message which we have heard of him, and declare unto you, that God is light, *r* and in him is no darkness at all.

6 If we say that we have fellowship with him, and walk in darkness, we lie, and do not the truth: *Jo. 8. 12. & 12. 46.*

Ps. 89. 15.
Jo. 11. 9.
7 But if we walk *t* in the light, as he is in the light, we have fellowship one with

v. 16. 30.
v. 2. 13.
another, and the blood *x* of Jesus Christ his Son cleanseth us from all sin. *He. 13. 12.*

v. 12. 8.
v. 15. 21, 22.
8 If we say that we have no sin, *y* we deceive ourselves, and the truth is not in us.

Jer. 3. 13.
Ze. 3. 4.
Je. 33. 8.
9 If we confess *z* our sins, he is faithful and just to forgive us *our* sins, and to cleanse *b* us from all unrighteousness. *Is. 6. 7.*

10 If we say that we have not sinned, we make him a liar, and his word is not in us.

This is a magnification of part of I John 1 in F.R.H.'s Bagster Bible that she read and studied at the end of her life.

ROYAL COMMANDMENTS.

MORNING THOUGHTS

FOR

The King's Servants.

BY

FRANCES RIDLEY HAVERGAL

" I will delight myself in Thy commandments."—Psalm 119:47.

"Knowing her intense desire that Christ should be magnified, whether
by her life or in her death, may it be to His glory
that in these pages she, being dead,
'Yet speaketh ! ' "

Taken from the Edition of *The Complete Works of Frances Ridley Havergal.*

David L. Chalkley, Editor   Dr. Glen T. Wegge, Associate Editor

ISBN 978-1-937236-07-6   Library of Congress: 2011939758

Book cover by Sherry Goodwin and David Carter.

PREFATORY NOTE.

" A ROYAL COMMANDMENT from Him!" Some of His Royal Commandments are made so "plain upon tables, that he may run that
readeth." Some are carved between the lines of the tablets of sacred history,
and flash out only as the candle of the Lord falls upon them. Some are engraved upon the gems of promise; and as we look closely into the fair colours
of each jewel that the hand of faith receives, we find that it is enriched by an
unerasable line of precept. But all are royal, for all are "from Him," our King.
And He has said, "If ye love Me, keep My commandments."

The aim of this little book is to lead His servants, morning by morning,
not only to keep, but to seek, recognise, and delight in His Royal Commandments, and it is sent forth with the prayer that every reader may be taught by
His good Spirit more of the happy "obedience of faith."

It is hoped that the little companion volume, *Royal Bounty, or Evening
Thoughts for the King's Guests*, may be a tiny "cup of cold water" to some of His
tired children when their day's work, or day's waiting, is over. Both are offered,
very gratefully and lovingly, to the readers of *My King* who have spread those
simple "Daily Thoughts" so far beyond the writer's expectation, with the earnest request that they will join in thanksgiving for the blessing which *has* been
given, and in prayer that even greater blessing may be sent with these little
books, for our Lord Jesus Christ's sake.

F. R. H.

CONTENTS.

Note: "The Great Reward" for the "Thirty-First Day" was the last item in *Royal Commandments*. Because extra pages are available in this new edition, these further items (not published in *Royal Commandments*) are added here at the end: two music scores and three poems by Frances Ridley Havergal.

ADDENDA

FIRST DAY.

Loving Allegiance.

"Master!"—John 20:16.

I THINK this is the very epitome of love. Love understands love; it needs no talk. Sunlight needs no paraphernalia of pipes, and wicks, and burners; it just shines out, direct and immediate. And the dewdrop flashes it back in the same way. The sparkle may be tiny, but it is true and immediate; it needs no vehicle.

Isaiah 43:1

"I have called thee by thy name." That was quite enough. The powerful sunshine of His love was focussed into that white beam of sevenfold light, and the whole soul was concentrated into the responsive love-flash, "Master!"

When that word has truly gone up from the soul to Christ, then we have felt what we can never put into any other words. It is the single diamond of soul-expression, and we have cast it at His feet for ever.

Psalm 16:2

He accepts it; for how wonderfully sweetly falls His direct answer, "Ye call Me Master and Lord: and ye say well; for so I am." Think of this seal of approval being set upon the name we so love to give Him. "Ye say *well*."

John 13:13

Matthew 23:8, 10

He reserves it to Himself, for He says, "One is your Master, even Christ." It is sacred to Him in all its depth of meaning. He has put His hand upon our offering, claiming it as only His own; and now it can never be another's. It includes the whole attitude of soul towards our beloved Lord.

1 Samuel 25:35

1. *Love.*—There is a great hush; we have not any words at all. We cannot even tell Him we love Him, because we are dazzled with a glimpse of His love, and overwhelmed with our unworthiness of it. Our eyes fill, and our bosom heaves. The tide has risen too high for verbal prayer or praise; we have to be "silent in love"—the very silence being an echo

2 Samuel 1:26;
Ephesians 3:19

Zeph. 3:17, margin

of the eternal depth of calmness of the exceeding great love in which He rests. There is only one word which does not jar with the still music of such a moment,—"Master!"

2. *Adoration.*—For the breathing of the name is all we can do to express the unexplainable recognition of His glory. Already He is "admired in all them that believe" with the admiration of astonishment. "We praise Thee, we bless Thee, we worship Thee, we glorify Thee, we give thanks to Thee for Thy great glory." And yet we only uttered the one word, "Master!"

3. *Allegiance.*—The true utterance of it is the very oath of allegiance. We cannot, must not, dare not, will not, henceforth serve "two masters," nor the still more subtle "many masters." The word has been breathed into His heart, and He will treasure it there, and keep it for us. It *has been said,* and the sound-waves can never be recalled; they will vibrate through the universe for ever. God grant that no traitorous whisper may ever cross them!

4. *Confidence.*—We have found One whom we can trust implicitly, and rest upon entirely. We have put our lives into His hand. We have burned the bridge behind us, because we are quite sure He is the Captain of our salvation. We have entered His service *for ever.* We have given our allegiance unreservedly, because we confide in Him unreservedly. There is no question about it. "I know whom I have believed," and therefore I say, "Master!"

5. *Obedience.*—All a mockery without this! Not only our lips, but our lives must say, "Master!" And by His own grace they shall say it; the name shall be emblazoned on every page of our lives. For Jesus Himself will "make it plain" upon our tablets, so "that he may run that readeth it." This is the test, the fruit, the manifestation of love. But oh, how sweet that we may fearlessly say the word which pledges us to it, knowing that the Master Himself will enable us to fill it up with the practical obedience which, above all things, we want so intensely to yield to Him! It is like throwing our alpenstock up to a higher ledge of rock, and then giving ourselves up to the strong arm of the guide to draw us up after it.

Ephesians 2:4

John 1:14
2 Thess. 1:10 (*Gr.*)

Matthew 6:24
James 3:1;
Isaiah 26:13

Ephesians 1:12

Hebrews 2:10
Exodus 21:6
1 Chron. 12:18
2 Timothy 1:12

Habakkuk 2:2
John 14:15;
2 Cor. 5:14, 15
Philippians 2:13
2 Cor. 9:8

1 Samuel 30:13
Mark 10:17
Romans 14:4
John 13:13
1 Cor. 12:3

Never shall we have to say, like the Amalekite's servant, "My master left me!" He is our *good* Master, our "*own* Master," and He will reveal to His weak servants all that He means in His own faithful endorsement of the name which His Spirit has taught us to call Him.

"O Master, at Thy feet
I bow in rapture sweet!
Before me, as in darkling glass,
Some glorious outlines pass
Of love, and truth, and holiness, and power;
I own them Thine, O Christ, and bless Thee for this hour."

SECOND DAY.

Seeking for His Commandments.

"Keep and seek for all the commandments of the Lord your God."—1 Chronicles 28:8.

Psalm 119:96
Psalm 119:35

Psalm 119:66, 73,
131,127,47,115,
176

Leviticus 4:27–35

Psalm 40:8

Deut. 10:13

IS not this precept too often halved? We acknowledge our obligation to keep, but what about *seeking for* all the commandments of the Lord our God? Are we doing this?

"Thy commandment is exceeding broad," and our horizon must be continually widening if He is making us to go in the path of His commandments. Even when, by His grace, we have been led to take the seven beautiful steps in that path mentioned in that grand gush of Bible love, the 119th Psalm, believing them, learning them, longing for them, loving them, delighting in them, keeping them, and not forgetting them, there remains yet this further step, *seeking for all of them.*

Perhaps we have even a little shrinking from this. We are afraid of seeing something which might be peculiarly hard to keep; it seems as if it might be enough to try to keep what commandments we have seen without seeking for still more, and as if seeing more to keep would only involve us in heavier obligations and in more failures to keep them. And we almost wish we had never seen this added command, forgetting that shedding of blood was needed for sin "through ignorance." But we have seen it, even if we never noticed it before; it is shown us to-day, and we have no alternative but obedience or disobedience to it.

Does not a loving child like to find out what its dear father wishes it to do? does it not feel sorry that it did not know all he wished in time to avoid doing just the contrary? How little we must love His will if we would rather not know it, lest it should clash with our own! Even to take the lowest ground, all His commandments are "for our good,"

Psalm 19:11

Deut. 32:47

and "in keeping of them there is great reward"; so that we are clearly missing unknown good or unknown reward by remaining in ignorance of any of them. Nay, more, "it is your life" to observe to do *all* the words of His law.

We need not fear being left to struggle with newly discovered impossibilities; for, with the light that reveals a command, the grace to fulfil it will surely be given. It is very humbling when the Spirit's light flashes upon some command of our God which we have never "observed," much less "done"; and yet it is a very gracious answer to the prayer, "Teach me to do Thy will."

Deut. 11:32;

15:5, etc.

Psalm 143:10

In reading His word, let us steadily set ourselves to seek for all His yet unnoticed commandments, noting day by day what we find; and thus knowing more of His will, will be a step towards doing more of it. Let us not be content with vaguely praying, "Lord, what wilt Thou have me to do?" but set to work to see what He has already *said* we are to do, and then, "Whatsoever He saith unto you, do it."

Acts 9:6;

Habakkuk 2:1

John 2:5

THIRD DAY.

Recognising His Commandments.

"And this is His commandment."—1 John 3:23.

Deut. 12:32
Deut. 6:24
2 Cor. 9:8; 12:9

WE may be quite sure of three things,—first, that whatever our Lord commands us, He really means us to do; secondly, that whatever He commands us is "for our good always"; and, thirdly, that whatever He commands us, He is able and willing to enable us to do, for "all God's biddings are enablings."

Psalm 119:4
James 2:10

But do we practically recognise all His commandments *as* commandments, and the breach of any one of them as sin? As we read each precept, let us solemnly say to ourselves, "This is His *commandment*"; and oh, what a touchstone of guilt will it be! How we shall see that what we have been excusing as infirmity and natural weakness which we could not help, and shortcomings with regard to impossible standards, has been all sin, transgression, disobedience, needing to be bitterly repented of, needing nothing

Hebrews 9:22

less than blood, the precious blood of Christ, for atonement and cleansing, needing nothing short of Omnipotence to

Isaiah 40:29

strengthen us against it.

Perhaps this is the sad secret of many a mourning life among God's children. They are calling sin by other names.

Hebrews 12:1, 2

They think it is only natural temperament and infirmity, for which they are to claim sympathy, to go on doubting and

1 John 3:23

distrusting their Saviour and their God; yet "*this* is His commandment, That we should believe on the name of His Son Jesus Christ," and *this,* "Trust in Him at all times." They

Psalm 62:8

think they are to be tenderly pitied for having such a burden to bear, and such sadness of heart; yet *this* is His command-

Psalm 55:22
Philippians 4:4

ment, "Cast thy burden upon the Lord"; and *this,* "Rejoice in the Lord alway." They do not think they can exactly help

Matthew 22:37

their hearts being so cold that they do not know whether they love Him or not; yet *this* is His commandment, "Thou shalt love the Lord thy God with all thy heart." They almost feel as if their state were a rather interesting one.

Yet, oh! dear friend, if the Lord has indeed commanded these things, it is a state of disobedience. If He has said them, He *means* you to do them. Oh, come face to face with His word; do not shrink from the terrible shock of seeing *sin*

John 12:48

where you only thought of infirmity. It is by the word that He has spoken that you will be judged, not by man's excusing euphemisms. You are committing sin in doubting Him; you are directly disobedient in not trusting Him, not casting your burden upon Him, not rejoicing alway in Him; you

Matthew 22:38
James 2:10, 11

are a transgressor of His "first and great commandment" in not loving Him. "Thou art become a transgressor of the law," "guilty of all."

Oh! if the Holy Spirit flashes the light which He only can flash upon these commandments, and shows you the sins which, child of God though you are, you have never yet recognised as such, you cannot and will not rest in them, if indeed "the root of the matter is found" in you. It will

Job 19:28

wring from you an agony cry of "Lord, have mercy upon me, and incline my heart to keep *this* law," as He turns that terrible and yet merciful light on each. If you do not yet "see it quite so strongly," ask that blessed Spirit to show you, at any cost, what He has, sooner or later, to show you. For He will not show you the sin without the remedy. And never will the precious blood of Christ have been *so* precious to you as when, after such an entirely startling revelation of the guilt of your position of disobedience, you come,

1 John 1:9
Hebrews 13:12
Revelation 12:11
Psalm 119:60
Psalm 119:6

despairing of yourself, to the Fountain, and find the cleansing and sanctifying and overcoming power of the blood of the Lamb.

In that power make haste and delay not to keep His commandments, and then shall you not be ashamed when you have respect unto ALL His commandments.

FOURTH DAY.

———

The Means of Growth.

"Grow in grace, and in the knowledge of our Lord and Saviour Jesus Christ."
—2 Peter 3:18.

THE very thing we are longing to do, and perhaps mourning over not doing, and perhaps praying every day that we may do, and seeming to get no answer! But when God has annexed a means to the fulfilment of a command, we cannot expect Him to enable us to fulfil that command if we are not using His means. In this case the means are wrapped in another command: "Desire the sincere milk of the word, *that ye may grow* thereby."

1 Peter 2:2

Real desire must prove itself by action; it is no use desiring the milk and not drinking it. "Wherefore criest thou unto Me? speak unto the children of Israel, that they *go forward*." Let us to-day, and every day henceforth, "go forward," and use in faith and honest earnestness this His own great means of growth.

Exodus 14:15

By the word we shall "grow in grace." The beginning of grace in our souls was by the same; for it is written, "Of His own will begat He us with the word of truth"; "Being born again, ... by the word of God." At every step it is the same word which develops the spiritual life. The young man shall "cleanse his way" by it. The entrance of it giveth light and understanding. The result of hiding it in our hearts is, that we "might not sin against Thee"; and how often by His word has He "withheld thee from sinning against Me!" Again and again we have said, "Thy word hath quickened me." For it comes to us "not in word only, but in power and in the Holy Ghost, and in much assurance." It is "able to make thee wise unto salvation," and its intended effects of reproof, correction, instruction in righteousness, rise to

James 1:18
1 Peter 1:23

Psalm 119:9
Psalm 119:130
Psalm 119:11

Genesis 20:6
Psalm 119:50
1 Thess. 1:5
2 Timothy 3:15

2 Timothy 3:16

what would seem a climax of growth, "that the man of God may be perfect, throughly furnished unto *all* good works." And yet there is a still more glorious result of this "word of God, which effectually worketh also in you that *believe*"; for by "His divine power" "are given unto us exceeding great and precious promises, that *by these* ye might be partakers of the divine nature." This is indeed the climax, for what can rise beyond this most marvellous effect of this blessed means of growth in grace! Oh, to use it as He would have us use it, so that every day we "may grow thereby"!

By the word we shall also grow in the knowledge of Christ. The mere surface of this is obvious. For how do we come to know more of any one whom having not seen, we love? Is it not by reading and hearing what he has said and written and done? How *are* we to know more of Jesus Christ, if we are not taking the trouble to know more of His word?

He hath said, "Search the Scriptures; for … they are they which testify of Me." Are we really searching, or only superficially reading, those Old Testament Scriptures of which He spoke? He says they testify of Him, *i.e.* tell us all about Him; are we acting as if we quite believed that?

"Beginning at Moses and all the prophets, He expounded unto them in ALL the Scriptures the things concerning Himself." Then there are things about Jesus in *all* the Scriptures—not just only in the Psalms and Isaiah, but in every book! How very much there must be for us to find! Let us ask the Holy Spirit to take of *these* things of Jesus and show them unto us, that we may grow in "the knowledge of the Son of God."

"The words which I speak unto you, they are spirit, and they are life"—quickening and continually lifegiving words. We want to be permeated with them; we want them to dwell in us richly, to be the inspiration of our whole lives, the very music of our spirits, whose melodious overflow may be glory to God and goodwill to man. Jesus Himself has given us this quick and powerful word of God, and our responsibility is tremendous. He has told us distinctly what to do as to it; He has said, "Search!" Now, are we substituting a word of

Marginal references:

2 Timothy 3:17

1 Thess. 2:13

2 Peter 1:3, 4

1 Peter 1:8

John 5:39

Luke 24:27

John 16:15
Ephesians 4:13

John 6:63

Colossians 3:16

Luke 2:14
John 17:14

John 5:39

Isaiah 34:16

our own, and merely *reading* them? He did not say, "Read
them," but "*Search!*" and it is a most serious thought for
many a comfortable daily *reader* of the Bible, that, if they are
only reading and not searching, they are distinctly living in
disobedience to one of His plainest commands. What wonder if they do not "grow thereby"!

> Let me then be always growing,
>   Never, never standing still,
> Listening, learning, better knowing
>   Thee, and Thy most blessed will;
> That the Master's eye may trace,
> Day by day, my growth in grace.

FIFTH DAY.

Mental Food.

"Eat ye that which is good."—Isaiah 55:2.

Psalm 73:22   "SO foolish was I, and ignorant: I was as a beast before Thee," or this commandment would not have been needed. Good, wholesome, delicious food set plentifully before us, and yet we have to be told to eat that which is good, and to let rubbish and poison alone! Is it not humiliating?

Romans 6:21
Isaiah 44:20
Hosea 12:1
Proverbs 15:14
Hosea 4:10
Micah 6:14
1 Peter 2:3

We know too much about feeding on that which is not good, and what profit had we in those things whereof we are now ashamed? The Lord has had to testify of us, "He feedeth on ashes," "feedeth on wind," "feedeth on foolishness." Most gracious was His decree, "They shall eat, and not have enough"; "Thou shalt eat, but not be satisfied." He would not *let* us be satisfied. And now, if we have tasted that the Lord is gracious, we *cannot* be satisfied with the old ashes and wind.

Matthew 4:4

But what about our daily practical obedience to this command? How much are we going to eat to-day of that which is good, in proportion to that which satisfieth not? Will it be a question of minutes for the word by which we live, and hours for books which are at best negative as to spiritual nutriment? What is our present obedience to the

1 Peter 2:2
Hebrews 5:12, 14
1 Cor. 2:10
Job 23:12

2 Timothy 2:21

Ezekiel 3:3

parallel command, "*Desire* the sincere milk of the word, that ye may grow thereby"? What about our appetite for the "strong meat," "the deep things of God"? If other books contain "necessary food" mentally, and we are called to use them, so that by study of His works, His providences natural, mental, moral, we may be more meet for the Master's use, do we practically and consciously esteem the words of His mouth *more*? Can we say, they are "in my mouth as honey for sweetness"?

But perhaps we are even purposing to eat that which is *not* good. We may argue that there is no harm in certain readings, and that if we don't read what others do we shall get narrow and lose conversational influence, and that people will think nothing of our opinion if we can't say we have read such and such books, and so forth. But all the time, do we not know, down in our heart of hearts, that this is all sophistry? We *know,* though we do not like to acknowledge, that the books in question do blunt our spiritual appetite and hinder our close communion with Jesus; that the influence we profess to want is not purely desired "for Jesus' sake only," and to be used "*all* for Jesus,"—in short, we *like* the reading, and we do not want to resist pleasing ourselves. And so we deliberately disobey the command to eat that which is good, excusing ourselves by pretending that we "saw that the tree was good for food," when the truth was that we simply saw that it was "pleasant."

We are solemnly responsible for the mental influences under which we place ourselves. "Take heed what ye hear" must include "take heed what ye read." "Lead us not into temptation" is "vain repetition" when we walk straight away into it, hoodwinking our own eyes because we are drawn away and enticed by our own desires.

Do we feel that we are not strong enough to resist? "The way of the Lord is strength to the upright"; and His "way to escape" is, "Eat ye that which is good." Perhaps, if Eve had fully availed herself of God's permission, "Thou mayst freely eat," she would not have been so ready to disregard His prohibition. If we "eat in plenty" of "angels' food," of course we shall not care about the "onions and the garlick." Just fancy wanting *them!* When we are "satisfied," of course, there is no craving.

The devil is very fond of persuading us that we have "no leisure so much as to eat" when it is a question of Bible study. He never says that if we have a novel "of the earth, earthy," or a clever magazine of "modern thought" on hand! He knows better. He wants us not to "*let*" our souls delight themselves in fatness.

Job 13:7

John 12:9

Isaiah 2:6
Romans 15:1–3

Genesis 3:6

Mark 4:24
Matthew 6:7, 13

James 1:14

Proverbs 10:29
1 Cor. 10:13
Genesis 2:16

Joel 2:26; Ps.78:25
Numbers 11:5
Jeremiah 31:14

Mark 6:31
1 Cor. 15:47

Isaiah 55:2

Proverbs 9:5
Song. 5:1

1 Kings 19:5

Isaiah 25:6
John 4:34
Leviticus 22:7

Revelation 2:7, 17
John 6:51, 57

Jesus, our Wisdom, says, "Come, eat of *My* bread"; "Eat, O friends." One is utterly ashamed that it should ever be an effort to obey this loving invitation. How weak we are! But His hand touches us, and He says, "Arise, and eat." May He open our eyes to see and rejoice in the provision so close beside us, the feast that He has made for us.

Not only His word, but the happy doing of His will shall be our meat, and we shall "afterward eat of the holy things, because it is His food." He will give us to eat of the tree of life and of the hidden manna. And He will give us Himself, the living Bread which came down from heaven, saying, "He that eateth Me, even he shall live by Me." Is not this enough?

SIXTH DAY.

The Transferred Burden.

"If our transgressions and our sins be upon us, and we pine away in them, how should we then live?"—Ezekiel 33:10.

Psalm 38:4

I F they are upon us, how can we live? For "mine iniquities are ... as an heavy burden they are too heavy for
me." "The burden of them *is* intolerable." It is not the sense,
but the burden itself which cannot be borne; no one *could*
bear his own iniquities without being sunk lower and lower,
and at last to hell by it. It is only not felt when the very elas-
ticity of sin within us keeps us from feeling the weight of the
sin upon us; as the very air in our bodies prevents our feeling the otherwise crushing weight of the atmosphere with its
tons upon every inch. Or (thank God for the alternative!)
when the whole burden, our absolutely intolerable burden,
is known to be laid upon another.

Romans 6:4
Psalm 119:32
Isaiah 9:1

If this burden is upon us, we cannot walk in newness of
life, we cannot run in the way of His commandments, we
cannot arise and shine. The burden is "too heavy" for these
manifestations of life; we do but "pine away" in our sins,
whether consciously or unconsciously; and the sentence is

Ezekiel 4:17
Leviticus 5:17

upon us. They shall "consume away for their iniquity." For
there is no curse so terrible and far-reaching as, "He shall
bear his iniquity."

Isaiah 53:6

"If!" but *is* it? It is written, "The Lord hath laid on
Him the iniquity of us all." On Jesus it has been laid, on
Him who alone could bear the intolerable burden; therefore

Isaiah 53:11

it is *not* upon His justified ones who accept Him as their sin-
bearer.

Leviticus 16:22

This burden is never divided. He took it *all*, every item,
every detail of it. The scapegoat bore "upon him *all* their in-

iquities." Think of every separate sin, each that has weighed down our conscience, every separate transgression of our most careless moments, added to the unknown weight of all the unknown or forgotten sins of our whole life, and all this laid on Jesus instead of upon us! The sins of a *day* are often a burden indeed, but we are told in another type, "I have laid upon thee the *years* of their iniquity." Think of the *years* of our iniquity being upon Jesus! Multiply this by the unknown but equally intolerable sin-burdens of all His people, and remember that "the Lord hath laid on Him the iniquity of us *all*," and then think what the strength of His enduring love must be which thus bear "the sins of *many*."

Think of His bearing them "in His own body on the tree," in that flesh and blood of which He took part, with all its sensitiveness and weakness, because He would be made like unto His brethren in all things; and that this bearing was entirely suffering (for He "*suffered* for sins"), and praise the love which has not left "our sins ... upon us."

We cannot lay them upon Him; Jehovah has done that already, and "His work is perfect:" "nothing can be put to it, nor anything taken from it." "The Lord *hath* laid on Him the iniquity of us all"; "He hath done this." We have only to look up and see our Great High Priest bearing the iniquity of our holy things for us; to put it still more simply, we have only to believe that the Lord has really done what He says He has done.

Can we doubt the Father's love to us, when we think what it must have cost Him to lay that crushing weight on His dear Son, sparing Him not, that He might spare us instead? The Son accepted the awful burden, but it was the Father's hand which "laid it upon" Him. It was death to Him, that there might be life to us. For "if our transgressions and our sins" were upon us, there could be no answer to the question, "How should we *then* live?" for we could only "pine away in them" and die. "Ye shall die in your sins." But being "laid on Him," how shall we *now* live? "He died for all, that they which live should not henceforth live unto themselves, but unto Him which died for them

Ezekiel 4:5

John 1:29
Isaiah 53:6
John 13:1
Hebrews 9:28
1 Peter 2:24
Hebrews 2:14, 17

1 Peter 3:18

Deut. 32:4
Eccl. 3:14; Is. 53:6
Psalm 22:31
Exodus 28:38

Isaiah 44:23

John 3:16

Rm. 8:32; Mal. 3:17
1 Peter 2:24
Genesis 22:6
1 Thess. 5:10

John 8:24
2 Cor. 5:15

Rm. 14:8; Gal. 2:20 | and rose again." Unto Him, by Him, in Him, for Him,
Phil. 1:21; Jn.17:24 | now; and with Him, where He is, for ever and ever!
1 Thess. 4:17

On Thee, the Lord

Amos 5:12   My mighty sins hath laid;
Zechariah 13:7   And against Thee Jehovah's sword

Flashed forth its fiery blade.

Isa. 53:8, margin   The stroke of justice fell on Thee,
1 Chron. 21:17   That it might never fall on me.

SEVENTH DAY.

The Recall.

"O Israel, return unto the Lord thy God; for thou hast fallen by thine iniquity."
—Hosea 14:1.

Hosea 2:6

THANK God that He does not let His children go on comfortably when they wander and fall!

Have we not known (God grant we may never again know!) a wretched mental nausea, a sense of discomfort and restlessness, a misgiving that something is wrong, though we can't say what? no actual pain, no acute attack of anything, but a nameless uncomfortableness, most easily described by a negative, that we are *not* "as in months past."

Job 29:2
Job 15:11, 12

If this is the present state of any reader, do let me most earnestly and affectionately entreat you not to remain one day - no, not one hour - in this most dangerous state, the beginning of backsliding, and already a fall from your "own stedfastness" and your "first love." "Remember from whence thou art fallen"; look unflinchingly at your position, and recognise frankly the difference between to-day, and the past days of closer walking and happy abiding. Do not let yourself drift on, or you "will revolt more and more" till "the whole head is sick, and the whole heart faint." Every day's delay will make your case worse.

2 Peter 3:17
Revelation 2:4, 5

Isaiah 1:5

Do not shrink from asking Him to show you how and why it is that you have fallen. The "beautiful crown" which He put "upon thine head" in "the time of love," would not have "fallen from our head," but "that we have sinned." It is "by *thine* iniquity" that "thou art fallen," —iniquity personal and real, though very likely unguessed by any one, and hidden even from thine own eyes.

Ezekiel 16:12
Ezekiel 16:8
Lament. 5:16
Hosea 14:1

Perhaps the knowledge of this is already sent; if so, listen! "And I said, *after* she had done all these things, Turn

Jeremiah 3:7

Jeremiah 3:1
Isaiah 55:7

Job 36:9, 10

Hosea 14:1
Jeremiah 3:12
Isaiah 44:22
Psalm 116:7
Hosea 6:1

Isaiah 30:18
Acts 24:25

Psalm 116:7
Hos. 14:1; Ps. 67:6
Hosea 2:19
Psalm 135:4

Jeremiah 2:2
Hosea 11:8

Hosea 2:7

Jeremiah 4:1
2 Samuel 3:18
Jeremiah 18:11

Psalm 65:4
Jeremiah 30:3
Hos. 13:9;
Lam. 5:21; Lk.
15:22, 25
Job 22:23–28

thou unto me." And again, though you may have gone after other "lovers," "*yet* return again to me, saith the LORD." Oh forsake the *thoughts* as well as the way, and return unto the Lord, and He will abundantly pardon. For when "He showeth them their work and their transgressions," He also "*commandeth* that they return from iniquity."

And why? Five infinitely gracious reasons are given. "Return! ... *for* thou hast fallen by thine iniquity"; the very thing which seemed the barrier to return! "Return! ... *for* I am merciful, saith the LORD." "Return! ... *for* I have redeemed thee." "Return! ... *for* the Lord hath dealt bountifully with thee." "Come, and let us return unto the Lord: *for* He hath torn, and He *will* heal us." All these gracious words for you! and the Lord Himself waiting that He may be gracious! Will you keep Him waiting till a more "convenient season"?

To *whom* are you called to return? Ah! think of *that* —not to a state or position merely; not only "to thy rest," but to "the Lord thy God"; *thy* God, "our *own* God"; to Him who has betrothed you unto Him for ever; to Him who chose you unto Himself to be His peculiar treasure; to Him who remembers better than you do from whence you have fallen. Hear Him saying, "I remember thee, the kindness of thy youth, the love of thine espousals." "How shall I give thee up?" What pathetic yearning this is over you, even you! Will you not say, "I will go and return to my first husband; for then was it better with me than now."

Is intention enough in this matter? Listen again to the arousing words of your Lord, "If thou *wilt* return, ... saith the Lord, *return* unto Me"; in other words, "Now, then, *do* it." Stay no more at being willing to return, but "*Return ye* NOW!" It will be harder to-morrow—nay, harder an hour hence than now. He who first caused you to approach, will cause you to return; so you shall not be left unaided, for "In Me is thine help" even for returning from self-destruction.

And then—oh, what wealth of promises to the returning one! what robes and rings and heavenly music! "If thou return, ... thou shalt be built up, thou shalt put away iniquity ...; then shalt thou have thy delight in the Almighty,

and shalt lift up thy face unto God ... He shall hear thee, ...
Thou shalt decree a thing, and it shall be established unto
thee: the light shall shine upon thy ways." For He hath said,
"I will heal their backsliding, I will love them freely."

Hosea 14:4

Return!
O fallen; yet not lost!
Canst thou forget the life for thee laid down,
The taunts, the scourging, and the thorny crown?
When o'er thee first my spotless robe I spread
And poured the oil of joy upon thy head,
How did thy wakening heart within thee burn!
Canst thou remember all, and wilt thou not return?

EIGHTH DAY.

The Conditions of Effectual Prayer.

"And all things, whatsoever ye shall ask in prayer, believing, ye shall receive."
—Matthew 21:22.

Mark 12:24

HAVE we not sometimes been tempted to think that here, at least, is a case in which our Lord has not literally and always kept His word? in which we do not get quite so much as the plain English of the promise might lead us to expect? If so, well may He say to us, "Do ye not therefore err, because ye know not the Scriptures, neither the power of God?" If we had known the Scriptures by searching, we might have known more of the power of God by experience in this matter. For this is no unconditional promise; this marvellous "whatsoever" depends upon five great conditions; and, if we honestly examine, we shall find that every case of seeming failure in the promise can be accounted for by our own failure in one or more of these.

John 14:6, 13
Phil. 2:10 (Gr.)

1 John 2:1

1. "Whatsoever ye shall ask *in my name,* that will I do." Really, not verbally only, in the name of Jesus; asking not in our own name at all; signing our petition, as it were, with His name only; coming to the Father by our Advocate, our Representative. Do we always ask thus?

Matthew 21:22
Hebrews 11:33

Romans 4:20

2. "*Believing,* ye shall receive." The faith-heroes of old "through faith ... obtained promises," and there is no new way of obtaining them. Is it any wonder that, when we stagger at any promise of God through unbelief, we do not receive it? Not that the faith merits the answer, or in any way earns it or works it out, but God has made believing a condition of receiving, and the Giver has a sovereign right to choose His own terms of gift.

John 15:7

3. "*If ye abide in Me, and My words abide in you,* ye shall ask what ye will, and it shall be done unto you." Ah! here

James 4:3

is a deeper secret of asking and *not* having, because we ask amiss. Not, have we come to Christ? but, are we abiding in Him?—not, do we hear His words? but, are they abiding in us? Can we put in this claim to the glorious "whatsoever"? And, if not, why not? for "*this* is His commandment," "Abide in Me." And this leads us to see the root of our failure in another condition, for,—

John 15:4

1 John 3:22
Psalm 66:18
John 15:4

2 Cor. 5:7
Hebrews 11:6

4. "Whatsoever we ask, we receive of Him, *because we keep His commandments, and do those things that are pleasing in His sight.*" Only as we are abiding in Him can we bring forth the fruit of obedience, for without (*i.e.* apart from) Him we can do nothing; only in walking by faith can we do those things that are pleasing in His sight, for without faith it is impossible to please Him.

1 John 5:14
Ephesians 5:17

5. "If we ask anything *according to His will,* He heareth us." When what we ask is founded on a promise or any written evidence of what the will of the Lord is, this is comfortingly clear. But what about petitions which may or may not be according to His will? Surely, then, the condition can only be fulfilled by a complete blending of our own will with His; by His so taking our will, so *undertaking* it and influencing it for us, that we are led to desire and ask the very thing He is purposing to give. *Then,* of course, our prayer is answered; and the very pressure of spirit to pray becomes the pledge and earnest of the answer, for it is the working of His will in us.

Philippians 2:13

Two comforting thoughts arise.

First, the very consciousness of our failure in these great conditions shows us the wonderful kindness and mercy of our King, who has answered so many a prayer in spite of it, according to His own heart, and not according to our fulfilment, giving us "of His royal bounty" that to which we had forfeited all shadow of claim.

2 Samuel 7:21

1 Kings 10:13

Secondly, that He who knoweth our frame knows also the possibilities of His grace, and would never tantalize us by offering magnificent gifts on impossible conditions. "Will he give him a stone?" Would an earthly parent? Would *you?* Therefore the very annexing of these intrinsically most blessed conditions implies that His grace *is* suffi-

Psalm 103:14
Philippians 4:13

Luke 11:11

2 Cor. 12:9

1 John 2:27
Colossians 1:10
cient for their fulfilment, and should lure us on to a blessed life of faith, abiding in Jesus, walking in obedience "unto *all* pleasing," and a will possessed by His own divine will.

> Thou art coming to a King,
> Large petitions with thee bring;
> For His grace and power are such,
> None can ever ask too much.
>
> NEWTON.

NINTH DAY.

The Privilege of Intercession.

"Pray one for another."—James 5:16.

Esther 1:19
1 Timothy 2:1
Hebrews 7:25
Romans 1:31
Ephesians 2:12

Deut. 33:23
Matthew 15:13

HERE our divine Master takes up an impulse of natural affection, raising it to the dignity of a "royal commandment," and broadening it to the measure of His own perpetual intercession. For, unless a heart has reached the terrible hardening of being "without natural affection" as well as "without God," it must want to pray for those it loves. The Lord would sanctify and enlarge this impulse, making it "full of the blessing of the Lord." It is a plant which He hath planted in the human heart, and therefore it shall not be rooted up, but He will water and increase it. What are the indications of His will in the matter, and how far are we following them out?

James 5:16
Genesis 20:17

Hosea 11:3
Mark 5:29, 33
Luke 17:15

Psalm 103:1–3

First, are we asking for each other the special thing annexed to the command? "That ye may be healed." Prayer for physical healing is clearly included. How many around us are not spiritually healed! are we definitely asking this for them? Of how many of His own people is the Lord saying, "They knew not that I healed them!" Not "knowing what was done in" them, they are not witnessing to the power of the Healer; not *seeing*, like the Samaritan, that they were healed, they are not giving Him thanks. Are we asking that they may realize the healing, so that they may glorify the Healer?

2 Cor. 1:11
Daniel 2:17, 18
Esther 4:16
Mt. 18:19; Ecc. 4:9
Exodus 17:11, 12

We may be greatly "helping together by prayer," by agreement in intercession. The very fact of having "agreed" is a great stimulus and reminder. It is the Lord's own indicated way. "Two of you." It took two to hold up Moses' hands steadily. When he let down one hand, Amalek prevailed. So Aaron and Hur were both wanted.

Intercession should be definite and detailed. Vagueness is lifelessness. St. Paul besought the Romans to pray for him, and then told them exactly what he wanted, four definite petitions to be presented for him. It is a help to reality of intercession when ministers or other workers who ask our prayers will tell us exactly what they want. General prayers for "blessing" are apt to become formal.

We must not yield to the idea that, because we are feeble members, doing no great work, our prayers "won't make much difference." It may be that this is the very reason why the Lord keeps us in the shade, because He hath need of us (though we feel no better than an "ass's colt") for the work of intercession. Many of us only learn to realize the privilege of being called to this by being called apart from all other work. When this is the case, let us simply and faithfully do it, "lifting up holy hands, without wrath and doubting," blessing His name who provides this holy and beautiful service for those who "*by night* stand in the house of the Lord." See how wonderfully St. Paul valued the prayers of others. He distinctly expresses this to every Church but one to whom he wrote. Would he have asked their prayers so fervently if he thought it would not "make much difference"?

Intercession is a wonderful help to forgiveness of injuries. See how the personal unkindness of brother and sister stirred up Moses to pray for each; and how repeatedly the wrong feeling, speaking, and acting of the people against himself was made the occasion of prayer for them. Let us avail ourselves of this secret of his meekness. Also it is an immense help to love. Do we not find that the more we pray for any one, the more we love?

Let us intercede "while we have time." "The night cometh, when no man can work." Those for whom we might be praying to-day may be beyond the reach of prayer to-morrow. Or our own day of prayer may have passed; for the only intercession that we have ever heard from the other side was in vain—never granted.

It is considerable practical help if we make our intercession systematic, especially if the Lord gives us many to pray for. If every day has its written list of special names

Side notes: Romans 15:30, 32 — 1 Cor. 12:22 — Mark 11:2, 3; Job 11:12 — Mark 6:31 — 1 Timothy 2:8 — Psalm 134:1; 2 Cor. 1:11; Eph. 6:19; Phil. 1:19; Col. 4:3; 1 Th. 5:25; Heb. 13:18, etc. — Num. 12:2, 13; Deut. 9:18–20 — Num. 14:2, 19; 16:19, 22; 12:3 — Gal. 6:10 (old translation); John 9:4 — Luke 16:27–31

to be remembered, we shall be less likely to forget or drop
them. Each several name was engraved on the breastplate
of the high priest, that it might be borne upon his heart
continually.

Exodus 28:21, 29

See the two-fold rewards of intercessory prayer.

First, blessing for others:

"He shall ask, and He shall give him life for them that
sin not unto death." Compare St. Paul's prayers for the Thes-
salonians, in his First Epistle, with the exact and abounding
answers for which he gives thanks in the Second, after a very
short interval.

1 John 5:16
1 Thess. 3:10, 12
2 Thess. 1:3, 4

Secondly, blessing for ourselves:

"The Lord turned the captivity of Job, *when* he prayed
for his friends." Something very like a turning of our captivity is granted when, amid oppression and darkness, we pray
for our friends. Often it is like a leap into the free sunshine.
"Pray unto the Lord for it" (the city whither they were carried away), "for in the peace thereof shall ye have peace."
Specially true is it in this, that "he that watereth shall be wa-
tered also himself."

Job 42:10
Psalm 126:1–3

Jeremiah 29:7

Proverbs 11:25

"O Saviour Christ, their woes dispel;
　　For some are sick, and some are sad,
And some have never loved Thee well,
　　And some have lost the love they had.

And some are pressed with worldly care,
　　And some are tired with sinful doubt,
And some such grievous passions tear
　　That only Thou canst cast them out.

And some have found the world is vain,
　　Yet from the world they break not free;
And some have friends that give them pain,
　　Yet have not sought a Friend in Thee."

HENRY TWELLS.

TENTH DAY.

———

Trusting in Darkness.

"Who is among you that feareth the Lord, that obeyeth the voice of His servant, that walketh in darkness, and hath no light? let him trust in the name of the Lord, and stay himself upon his God."—Isaiah 50:10.

Isaiah 48:18
Deut. 11:8

Job 15:4
Psalm 111:10
Isaiah 33:6
Psalm 119:69
Joshua 24:24
John 3:20
1 John 2:11

Exodus 34:6, 7

Isaiah 9:6

Matthew 1:21
Psalm 9:10
Psalm 119:55
Psalm 48:12, 13
Proverbs 18:10

Psalm 20:7
Matthew 6:6
Romans 8:26

BEFORE we take this peace and strength-giving precept, with its enfolded promise, to ourselves, let us examine ourselves as to the conditions: fear of the Lord, and obedience to the voice of His servant. They are very clear. If we are not casting off fear; if we have this "beginning of wisdom," this perhaps not sufficiently recognised "treasure," the fear of the Lord; and if we have sincerity of purpose about obeying the voice of His servant, and are not persisting in some known and wilful disobedience, which causes a different kind of darkness, the darkness that blindeth our eyes, then we are called to listen to all the comfort of this commandment.

"Let him trust in the name of the Lord." What name? "The Lord, the Lord God, merciful and gracious, long-suffering, and abundant in goodness and truth, keeping mercy for thousands, forgiving iniquity and transgression and sin." What name? "Wonderful, Counsellor, the Mighty God, the Everlasting Father, the Prince of Peace." What name? Just this, JESUS! But how can we trust in what we do not much consider? Trust needs a very broad and strong foundation for its repose; it cannot poise itself on an inverted pyramid. But if we walk about that foundation, and go round about it, and mark well the bulwarks, we shall put ourselves in the way of realizing what reason we have to trust.

Is it dark now, dear friend? Will you, as a little child, simply do what I ask you this morning? Take this *Name* of the Lord, in all its varied fulness, "shut thy door," and kneel down without hurry. Then, asking first the Spirit's prom-

Zechariah 12:10

Isa. 12:2; Ps. 91:2;
Ps. 31:1; Song. 1:3

John 12:46
Psalm 112:4

John 8:12

John 20:29
Psalm 2:12
Psalm 84:12
Psalm 23:4

Jeremiah 17:7
Isaiah 26:3

Isaiah 26:4

Ephesians 5:1
John 20:29
Psalm 33:21

ised help, pray over every separate part of it as so beautifully revealed for our comfort. And as you take up each word in petition, tell the Lord that you *will*, you *do* trust that, even though you cannot see or feel all the preciousness of it.

Trusting in the name of the Lord, the Triune Jehovah—Father, Saviour, Comforter—will lead you on, not perhaps to any great radiance of light as yet, but to staying upon your God; for mark the added pronoun, first only "*the* Lord," then "*his* God." Both the trusting and staying may be at first in the dark, but they will not be always in the dark. He that believeth on Him shall not abide in darkness. Unto him "there ariseth light in the darkness." But the promises are progressive: we must follow the Light as soon as we see it, for "he that followeth Me shall not walk in darkness."

But, meanwhile, even the trusting and staying shall be blessed, for "blessed are they that have not seen, and yet have believed." "Blessed are all they that put their trust in Him"; and "all" of course includes you. There may be very much unconscious blessing apart from sensible light and joy. The visible, light-bearing rays of the spectrum are not the whole beam. It is not they which make the plant grow; it is the dark rays with their mysterious, unseen vibrations that bring heat and chemical power.

The first conscious blessing is not linked with even the trust, but with the "staying" which grows out of it. "Thou wilt keep him in perfect peace, whose mind is stayed on Thee: because he trusteth in Thee." Then, again, the staying, and the certainly resulting, because absolutely promised, peace lead on to fuller and more settled trust: "Trust ye in the Lord for ever."

How we do love a little child that nestles up to us from its cot in a dark room, and kisses the hand that it cannot see, and pours out all sorts of little confidences which it did not tell in the broad daylight! Do we not fondle it with a special gush of affection? However much we loved the little thing before, we think we love it more than ever! When the Father's little children come to Him in the dark, and simply believe His assurance that He is there, although they cannot see, will He be less loving, less kind and tender?

Job 23:8–10

"I cannot hear Thy voice, Lord,
　　But Thou dost hear my cry;
I cling to Thine assurance
　　That Thou art ever nigh.
I know that Thou art faithful;
　　I trust, but cannot see
That it is still the right way
　　By which Thou leadest me."

ELEVENTH DAY.

———

Fear Not.

"Fear not."—Luke 12:32, etc.

Isaiah 33:6
Acts 9:31
1 John 4:18

Genesis 42:21

Jeremiah 6:19

Exodus 20:15

Revelation 21:8

Genesis 3:10
Luke 19:21
2 Samuel 6:8, 9

THERE need be no difficulty in distinguishing between the holy and blessed "fear of the Lord," which is our "treasure," and which is only as the sacred shadow cast by the brightest light of love and joy, and the fear which "hath torment," and is cast out by perfect love and simple trust.

> "Fear Him, ye saints, and you will then
> Have nothing else to fear!"

precisely expresses the distinction.

But it is a very solemn thought how "verily guilty" we are as to this most absolute command of our King, reiterated by messengers angelic and human, and by His own personal voice, perhaps more often than any other. No wonder that we are left to suffer the fruit of our own thoughts when we do not even see our disobedience, much less cease from it. "Fear NOT." There is no qualification, no exception, no modification; it is as plain a command as, "Thou shalt *not* steal." What excuse have we for daring to regard it as a less transgression, or even no transgression at all? If the heinousness of a crime might, to human judgment, be measured by its penalty, what must the true heinousness of this everyday sin be when God hath said, "The *fearful* shall have their part in the lake which burneth with fire and brimstone!"

Why should what seems only a natural infirmity be catalogued with the blackest sins? Because, if we honestly examine it, it is always and only the fruit of not really believing God's words, not really trusting His love and wisdom and power. It is a bold, "Yea, hath God said?" to His abundant

Isaiah 51:12, 13

John 16:8, 9
Romans 7:13
Psalm 119:175

Isa. 41:10; 43:1–5
Matthew 10:28
Lament. 3:57
Rev. 1:17; 2:10;
Isaiah 51:12, 13
Gen. 15:1; Matt.
14:27; Isa. 35:4;
Psalm 23:4

Psalm 27:1

Matt. 8:26; Rom.
1:20; Luke 1:74
Job 11:15

Jeremiah 23:4

Psalm 34:4
Hebrews 13:8

John 14:27

and infinitely gracious promises; it is a tacit denial that He is what He is! Only let us sincerely and thoroughly trace down every fear to its root, and we shall (if the Holy Spirit guide our search) be convinced of its sinfulness, and "by the commandment" it will "become exceeding sinful." "Let Thy judgments help" us, O Lord, in this matter.

But now for the brighter side! Would our King tell us again and again, "Fear not!" if there were any reason at all to fear? Would He say this kind word again and again, ringing changes as of the bells of heaven upon it, only to mock us, if He knew all the time that we could not possibly help fearing? Only give half an hour to seeking out the reasons He gives why we are not to fear, and the all-inclusive circumstances in which He says we are not to fear; see how we are to fear nothing, and no one, and never, and nowhere; see how He Himself is in every case the foundation and the grand reason of His command, His presence and His power always behind it; and then shall we hesitate to say, "I will fear *no* evil; for Thou art with me"? Shall we even fancy there is any answer to those grand and for ever unanswered questions, "The Lord is my light and my salvation; whom shall I fear? the Lord is the strength of my life; of whom shall I be afraid?"

There is a "Fear not" for every possible case and kind of fear; so that we have never any answer to give when He asks, "*Why* are ye fearful?" but we are "without excuse." It is part of His "holy covenant" that we should "serve Him without fear." It is one of His "precious promises" that "thou shalt be stedfast, and shalt not fear." It is one of the blessed results of His reign that His flock "shall fear no more." It is no impossible thing, but the simple and natural consequence of really seeking and really trusting the Lord, that He will deliver us not from some, but from "*all*" our fears. He did this for David, will He be less kind to you and me?

The Lord Jesus gives a very tender and gentle expression of the same command when He says, "Let not your heart be troubled, neither *let* it be afraid." Ah! we too often let our hearts be afraid: we yield without even a parley; a fear arises, and we do not recognise it as an enemy of our King, we just

Ephesians 6:17	*let* it enter and sit down, instead of unsheathing the sword
Ephesians 6:10	of the Spirit and attacking it in the power of His might, and
Psalm 44:5	in the Name that always conquers. No matter how power-
Luke 10:17	less we feel about it, strength comes with determination to
Mark 3:5	obey. Let us say this morning, *now,* "I *will* trust and *not* be
Isaiah 12:2	afraid"; and then let us "say to them that are of a fearful
Isaiah 35:4	heart, Be strong, fear not; ... He will come and save you."

Rom. 8:31; Ps. 56:9   Is God for me? I fear not, though all against me
  rise!

Psalm 3:6   When I call on Christ my Saviour, the host of evil
  flies.

My Friend, the Lord Almighty, and He who loves
  me—God!

1 Peter 3:13;   What enemy shall harm me, though coming as a
Isaiah 59:19   flood?

PAUL GERHARDT.

TWELFTH DAY.

The Strength-giving Look.

"And the Lord looked upon him, and said, Go in this thy might."—Judges 6:14.

Psalm 25:15

Jeremiah 24:6
Psalm 119:132
Job 33:27, 28;
Psalm 33:18, 19;
Psalm 32:8

Exodus 14:24

1 Samuel 16:7

Isaiah 5:2

Song. 7:12

Luke 22:61

Mark 9:24
Luke 9:38
Matthew 8:8

FOR the might of a look of the Lord is enough for anything! Only, we must meet His look; our eyes must be ever toward the Lord, and then we shall not miss it: for He says, "I will *set* Mine eyes upon them for good." So, if we are indeed His people, we can never look up to Him without His look of grace and goodness and guidance meeting ours.

It will not trouble us as it "troubled the Egyptians" when that mysterious look of the Lord fell upon them "through the pillar of fire and of the cloud"; that *look of judgment* is not for His Israel.

Yet for them there is the solemn *look of searching,* when He "looketh on the heart."

For them, too, the *look of expectation,* when He comes to His vineyard and looks "that it should bring forth grapes"; when He comes to "see if the vine flourish, whether the tender grape appear," with the beautiful promise in His hand, "There will I give thee My loves."

For them the unspeakable power and tenderness of His *look of recall.* One who, after denial of the faith, had felt the might of that look, said to a lad who stood awed by the manly tears: "Ah, Willie, it's forgiven sin that breaks a man's heart!" How many a wanderer has been called back even by the record that "the Lord turned, and looked upon Peter."

Then the *look of healing and help.* Have we as simple faith as the father who besought Jesus to *look* upon His only son, as if even a look from the dimly recognised Master should be enough? And so it was! the "word only," the

Mark 5:28
Mark 9:20, 21
Deut. 26:15

Mark 3:34
Matthew 12:49

Deut. 33:3
Luke 10:39

Judges 6:14

Psalm 32:8

Psalm 44:3
Psalm 71:16
Psalm 86:16
Psalm 68:28
Isaiah 45:24
2 Cor. 12:9

Isaiah 66:2
2 Samuel 9:8

2 Samuel 9:13

touch, the look, were enough for health and cure in cases to which this was a terrible climax.

Then the *look of blessing and love.* "Look down ... and bless Thy people," prayed Moses. And what a look of blessing that was when Jesus "looked round about on them which sat about Him," and "stretched forth His hand toward" them, and gave them the right of the nearest and dearest relationships! Oh! let us take time (*make* time, if need be) to "sit about Him" and listen to His teaching and meet His look.

And, last of the seven, there is for His people the special *look of strengthening.* There is so much in it. Suppose you are called to take part in some busy and complicated arrangements; it is all new to you; you are not quite sure you are doing the right thing in the right way; you hesitate and go on slowly and uncertainly, with no sense of freedom and power. All at once you catch the eye of the one who is leading and organizing! The look is enough; there is direction, approval, confidence, encouragement, in that one glance, and you work away altogether differently. Very graciously does the Master sometimes give this strengthening look—giving, in a way no one could convey to another, just what we needed for our special work. We know that our Lord has looked upon us, and the look has flashed electric strength into heart and hand; and we go on our way rejoicing, not at all in feeling any more able than before, but in the brightness of His power, saying, "I will go in the strength of the Lord God." And then His own strength is ours, and He says, "Go in this thy might," for "thy God hath commanded thy strength"; and yet we know more distinctly than ever that it is *His* strength which is made perfect in *our* weakness. Who is it that shall have the strengthening look of the Lord? "To this man will I look," saith Jehovah, "even to him that is poor and of a contrite spirit." It was he who said, "What is thy servant, that thou shouldest look upon such a dead dog as I am?" who "did eat continually at the king's table."

THIRTEENTH DAY.

All-sided Guidance.

"And guided them on every side."—2 Chronicles 32:22.

SEE the completeness of Jehovah's guidance! It is so different from human guidance. How seldom we feel that a human counsellor has seen our difficulty from every point of view, balanced all its bearings, and given guidance which will meet all contingencies, and be right not only on one side, but "on *every* side." But "His work is perfect" in this as in all other details; He will guide "when ye turn to the right hand, *and* when ye turn to the left." Perhaps we have gone about as Elymas did in his mist and darkness, "seeking some to lead him by the hand," putting confidence in earthly guides, and finding again and again that "it is not in man that walketh to direct his steps," and getting perplexed with one-sided counsels. Let us to-day put our confidence in His every-sided guidance.

Very often, the very recoil from an error lands us in an opposite one; because others, or we ourselves, have gone too far in one direction, we thenceforth do not go far enough, or *vice versa*: excess re-acting in defect, and defect in excess; a received truth overshadowing its equally valuable complementary one; the fear of overstepping the boundary line of the narrow track of truth and right, on the one side, leading us unconsciously to overstep it on the other side. But the promise which we should claim is, that the Holy Spirit would guide us into *all* truth, "*on every side.*"

How intensely restful is this completeness of guidance! There is nothing outside of God's all-inclusive promises about it. "I will direct *all* his ways." "I will direct their work in truth." Not only the general course, but "the *steps* of a good man are ordered by the Lord"; and what is less

Marginal references:

Deut. 32:4
Isaiah 30:21

Acts 13:11
Micah 7:5
Matthew 15:14
Jeremiah 10:23
Proverbs 3:6
Psalm 143:8
e.g.; John 13:8, 9
Acts 28:4, 6

John 16:13

Isa. 45:13; 61:8
Psalm 37:23

than a single step! Just realize this: every single little step of this coming day ordered by Jehovah! And lest you should sigh, "This is not for me, because I am not good," He repeats the same assurance still more simply: "The Lord directeth his steps." Now if we really believe these words, *need* we feel worried because we cannot see the steps ahead which Jehovah *is* going to direct, if we will let Him?

Proverbs 16:9

Isaiah 42:16

If we will let Him! Yes, this is no fatalistic leading. The guidance is conditional. He says, "I will guide thee with Mine eye"; but then we must look up to meet His eye. "Thou shalt guide me with Thy counsel"; but then we must listen for and listen to His counsel. "He shall direct thy paths"; but it is when we acknowledge Him in all our ways. He does not lead us whether or no!

Psalm 32:8
2 Chron. 20:12
Psalm 73:24
Proverbs 8:34
Proverbs 3:6

Suppose a little child is going with its father through an untracked wood. If it walks ever such a little way apart, it will make many a lost step; and though the father will not let it get out of sight and hearing, will not let it get lost, yet he may let it find out for itself that going just the other side of this tree leads it into a hopeless thicket, and stepping just the other side of this stone leads it into a muddy place, and the little steps have to be retraced again and again, till at last it asks the father to hold its hand, and *puts* and *leaves* its hand in his. Then, and not till then, there will be *no lost step,* for it is guided "on every side."

John 10:28

2 Chron. 32:31;
Deut. 8:2

Psalm 17:5
Psalm 31:3, 5
Proverbs 3:26
Proverbs 4:26,
margin

Need the little child go on a little longer by itself first? Had it not better put its hand into the father's at once? Will *you* not do so "from this time"? from this morning? Give up trying to pick your way; even if the "right paths" in which He leads you are paths that you have not known, say, "Even there shall Thy hand lead me." Let Him teach you *His* paths, and ask Him to make not your way, but "*Thy* way straight before my face." So shall you find the completeness and the sweetness of His guidance. For "the Lord shall guide thee continually," "by the springs of waters shall He guide" thee; He shall be the guide of your youth, and carry you even unto your old age; He will be your guide even unto death, and beyond: for one strain of the song of the victorious ones that stand upon the sea of glass mingled

Jeremiah 3:4
Proverbs 4:11;
Isaiah 42:16
Psalm 139:10
Psalm 25:4
Psalm 5:8
Isaiah 58:11
Isaiah 49:10
Jeremiah 3:4
Isaiah 46:4
Psalm 48:14
Revelation 15:2, 3

Exodus 15:13

with fire shall be, "Thou hast guided them in Thy strength unto Thy holy habitation."

> "I know not the way I am going,
> But well do I know my Guide;
> With a childlike trust I give my hand
> To the Mighty Friend at my side:
>
> And the only thing that I say to Him
> As He takes it, is: 'Hold it fast;
> Suffer me not to lose my way,
> And lead me home at last.'"

FOURTEENTH DAY.

___

Ruler, Because Deliverer.

"Rule thou over us, ... for thou hast delivered us."—Judges 8:22.

A LTHOUGH the passage in which these words occur cannot be considered a typical one, yet we may perhaps take them as illustrating and epitomizing the desire of every one whom Christ has delivered.

But what about this deliverance which precedes the prayer, "Rule thou over us"? Is it ours? Do we not know whether He has delivered us or not? It is no doing of ours, for "we have not wrought any deliverance." We have only His word about it, but that is indeed enough, in its absolute and unmistakable assurance: "Jesus, which delivered us from the wrath to come"; "Who *hath* delivered us from the power of darkness." This grand deliverance is accomplished, and Jesus Himself proclaims it. Will you doubt His own proclamation of His own act? He has opened the prison doors, and now bids the captives go free, and know that they are free. He has vanquished the foe and broken the bands of his yoke, and now tells you that He giveth you the victory which He has already won. What can He do more? He will do no more, because He has done all; therefore, if you do not accept the deliverance which He has wrought, there is no other for you, and "nothing can be put to it." Only believe it, and then you will joyfully say, "He hath delivered my soul in peace from the battle that was against me."

But you will not stop there. Merely to be "in peace" is not the end and aim of deliverance. If we are truly delivered, the Deliverer will soon be more to us than even the deliverance, and the gratitude and love will seek expression in obedience. Soldiers are ready to follow the captain who has won the victory anywhere and everywhere; they will not

Isaiah 38:17
Isaiah 26:18

1 Thess. 1:10
Colossians 1:13
Luke 4:18

Isaiah 42:7
Isaiah 61:1
Leviticus 26:13
1 Cor. 15:57
Coloss. 2:14, 15
Isaiah 44:23

Eccles. 3:14
Psalm 55:18

Luke 1:74

Luke 8:38, 39
Psalm 116:1, 8, 12

Rev. 14:4; 17:14

want to be in any other service, least of all in that of his foe.

We may take this as a test of the reality of our own participation in the deliverance which Christ has wrought for us. If we are saying, "Rule Thou over us," it is a sure proof that we may add, "for Thou hast delivered us"; for it is *His people* who are willing in the day of His power.

Psalm 110:3

This ruling is indeed the completion of the deliverance. It is not merely that the enemy is conquered and expelled from the stronghold, but that the citadel is occupied by a stronger than he; otherwise the garrison would be left headless and defenceless, and open at any moment to the fatal return of the foe. So the Saviour, who has redeemed our life from destruction, is the Jesus who shall save His people from their sins, who shall cast down imaginations, and bring every thought into captivity to the obedience of Christ. The Deliverer who comes to Zion is He who shall turn away ungodliness from Jacob. If we are not willing for this, we may well doubt whether we have any part or lot in the matter, and fear that we are yet in the bond of iniquity; for Christ will not arrange a partial salvation to meet our partial desire. He will not be our refuge from the penalty of sin, if we do not want Him as our refuge from the power. When the elders of Gilead turned to Jephthah in their distress, that he might lead them to victory over their oppressors, what was his condition?—"If ye bring me home again to fight against the children of Ammon, and the Lord deliver them before me, *shall I be your head?*"

Luke 11:22

Luke 11:26
Psalm 103:4
Matthew 1:21
2 Cor. 10:5

Isaiah 59:20
Romans 11:26
Acts 8:21, 23

Romans 6:1, 22
Titus 2:14
Judges 11:4–8

Judges 11:9

Acts 5:31
Psalm 56:13

Lord Jesus, Thou art exalted to be a Prince and a Saviour, and as such I need Thee and I desire Thee, "Thou hast delivered my soul from death," *therefore* I pray Thee to deliver my feet from falling, that I may "run the way of Thy commandments." Oh, sit and rule upon Thy throne in my heart; reign there until Thou hast put all enemies under Thy feet!

Psalm 119:32
Zechariah 6:13
1 Cor. 15:25

FIFTEENTH DAY.

Separation unto.

"Seemeth it but a small thing unto you, that the God of Israel hath separated you from the congregation of Israel, to bring you near to Himself?"—Numbers 16:9.

John 17:16;
1 John 2:15

Matthew 13:44
Romans 1:1

Matthew 4:19, 20

Mark 10:29, 30

Philippians 3:8;
1 Cor. 3:21–23
Psalm 45:15
Numbers 6:2
Ps. 4:3; Jn. 15:15
Proverbs 22:11

Psalm 148:14
Leviticus 20:26
Song. 7:10
Psalm 135:4
1 Kings 8:53
Titus 2:14
Numbers 6:8

Numbers 6:7

THE thought of separation, so inseparable from true and growing Christian life, is sometimes invested with an unnecessary sternness, because it is only viewed in one aspect. Young Christians are tempted to think "separation *from...*" a hard thing, because they do not see how it is far more than outweighed by "separation *unto.*" Let us think a little of this bright and beautiful side of it.

There is no true separation *from* the things which Jesus calls us to leave, without a corresponding separation *unto* things which are incomparably better. One hardly likes to speak of it as compensation, because the "unto" is so infinitely more than the "from"; it is like talking of a royal friendship compensating for dropping a beggar's acquaintance, or the whole Bank of England for a brass farthing, or palace life for "giving up" workhouse life!

First, and chiefly, we are separated unto the Lord Himself. He wants us not only for servants, but for friends; and He makes the friendship a splendid and satisfying reality. He wants to bring us "near to Himself," that we may be "a people near unto Him." He will not have a half possession in us, and so He says He hath "severed you from other people," why? "that ye should be Mine!" "chosen unto Himself," "His peculiar treasure," "separated from among all the people of the earth to be Thine inheritance." Is it "a small thing" thus to be the Lord's Nazarite, "holy unto the Lord all the days of his separation"? is any earthly crown to be compared to "the consecration (margin, separation) of his God upon his head"?

e.g. 1 Thess. 2:
17–20; 3:9;
2 John 1:12
Heb. 10:24, 25
2 Chron. 25:9
Neh. 10:28, 29
Mark 10:30
1 John 3:14
Psalm 133:1

Matthew 6:24
James 4:4

Hosea 7:8

Acts 13:2
Mark 13:34

Acts 27:23
Isaiah 52:11
Deut. 10:8
Psalm 134:1;
Job 35:10
Psalm 69:33
Matthew 25:40
1 Chron. 23:13

1 Cor. 1:26;
Philippians 3:14
Numbers 16:9

1 Cor. 2:9, 10

2 Cor. 6:17
1 John 3:23

John 14:3

We are separated also to far happier human friendships than the world knows. There is no isolation intended. "The Lord is able to give thee much more than this." Those who separated themselves *from* the people of the land *unto* the law of God, "*they* clave to their brethren." That is just it; we may lose "people," but we find "brethren," with all the love and pleasure and freedom of intercourse —yes, and even mirth—which that relationship brings. Is not this "much more" than the society of "*people*"?

But we do not get this, perhaps do not even guess its existence, as long as we try for both. Both means *neither,* in this case; we are conscious of the hollowness of the one, and we are not separated unto, and therefore cannot possibly know the enjoyment of, the other.

Then we are separated unto work, "*the* work whereunto I have called them"; very different kinds, but to every man his own work, and thereby an end of all the gnawing purposelessness, and downweighing uselessness, and miserable time-killing, and sense of helpless waste of life. *Ennui* is no part of a separated life; there is no room for that wretchedness any more. "Whose I am, and whom I serve," fills it up. Some are separated more especially "to bear the ark of the covenant of the Lord." Some only to stand before Him, it may be "by night," so that "songs in the night" may ascend to His glory. Some in a thousand ways "to minister unto Him," to His poor, to "His prisoners," spiritually or temporally; always "unto Him" in His representatives. But *all* "to bless in His name"; for praise is the invariable service of separation.

"Ye see your calling"; is it not a high one? "Seemeth it but a small thing to you?" Seemeth it too stern a thing? Is it not rather a "better thing" than fallen man could have dreamt of aspiring to? a brighter life than has entered into the natural heart of man even to imagine? Is it for *you*? Listen! "Be ye separate," and, what then? "*I* will receive you." "This is His commandment" to you, and this is His promise. Will you obey? Then you shall know a little, but every day more and more, of that unspeakable blessing of being "received" by the Father, until the day when Jesus

John 17:24 | shall come again and receive you unto Himself for the grand separation of eternity with Him.

> "As by the light of opening day
> The stars are all concealed,
> So earthly pleasures fade away
> When Jesus is revealed."
>
> JOHN NEWTON.

SIXTEENTH DAY.

Manifesting the Life of Jesus.

"That the life also of Jesus might be made manifest in our mortal flesh."
—2 Corinthians 4:11.

Phil. 3:14; 2 Tim. 1:9; Heb. 3:1 1 Peter 2:21	**I**S not this a "high" and "holy" and "heavenly" calling? Yet "even hereunto were ye called: because Christ also suffered for us, leaving us an example, that we should follow His steps." "Hereunto," to do just as He would have done, sometimes even just as He did do in like circumstances; to

IS not this a "high" and "holy" and "heavenly" calling? Yet "even hereunto were ye called: because Christ also suffered for us, leaving us an example, that we should follow His steps." "Hereunto," to do just as He would have done, sometimes even just as He did do in like circumstances; to show not our patience, but "the patience of Jesus Christ,"—not mere human meekness and gentleness, but "the meekness and gentleness of Christ," and so on with all the other beautiful and holy qualities which shone in "the life also of Jesus." While our "life is hid with Christ in God," His life is to be "manifest in our mortal flesh,"—yes, "magnified in my body."

"How shall this be?" First, Jesus Himself must dwell in our hearts by faith, or His life cannot be "manifest." He has said He will do so, but it is on conditions which He specifies: 1. Hearing His voice; 2. Opening the door to Him; 3. Loving Him; 4. Keeping His words. Not one of these can we fulfil without His grace, but not one of them will He deny us grace to fulfil, and the real desire to fulfil them is the beginning of that grace. Therefore let us "open unto Him immediately," and let Him come in and "abide with us," so that henceforth it may be, "Not I, but Christ liveth in me."

We want Him to make us vessels meet for this great use; pure and transparent vessels through which His glorious life may shine; so transparent, that, like clear glass, they may be altogether lost sight of in the light which streams through them; so pure, that they may not dim the radiance of His indwelling.

Side references:

Phil. 3:14; 2 Tim. 1:9; Heb. 3:1
1 Peter 2:21

Revelation 1:9
2 Cor. 10:1

Colossians 3:3
Philippians 1:20

Ephesians 3:17

Revelation 3:20
John 14:23
John 15:5
2 Cor. 12:9
Phil. 1:6; Luke 12:36; 24:29
Galatians 2:20
2 Timothy 2:21

The word "manifest" is more than mere showing; it implies a bringing to light, shining forth, and comes from the idea of a torch or lantern. We can only shine as lights in the world by bearing the Light of the World within us. But it is a grand and solemn responsibility. Our Lord Jesus is hidden from the eyes of the world; they do not see Him, they only see us, and our lives are to show them what His life is. What a tremendous trust our Master has given us! Who is sufficient for this thing? It is very real. He, our precious Lord, will be held in more or less esteem this day; His power, His grace, His sweetness will be judged of according to what the outsiders see in our lives. This day it rests with us to bring fresh reproach and discredit on His dear name, by caricaturing His life, or so truly to manifest it "that the name of our Lord Jesus Christ may be glorified in you."

Philippians 2:15
John 8:12
John 1:10
1 Peter 2:9, margin
2 Cor. 2:16
2 Cor. 4:7
2 Cor. 3:3
2 Thess. 1:12

> Thy life in me be shown!
> Lord, I would henceforth seek
> To think and speak
> Thy thoughts, Thy words alone,
> No more my own!

SEVENTEENTH DAY.

The Yoke-destroying Anointing.

"The yoke shall be destroyed because of the anointing." —Isaiah 10:27.

THE Assyrian yoke of old was not so real, so tangible, so continually felt a yoke, as that under which many a child of God is writhing; yet they are "called unto liberty," even "the glorious liberty of the children of God." And if the yoke of sin is felt to be real, the promised destruction of it surely will not be less so. If it is, as we know by sorrowful experience, no imaginary bondage, neither shall the deliverance be imaginary.

Galatians 5:13
Romans 8:21

You feel the yoke, but *how* shall it be destroyed? 1. Because of the grand anointing of our Lord Jesus Christ by God Himself "with the Holy Ghost and with power" to proclaim liberty to the captives; the grace and might of the Triune Jehovah thus combining in the proclamation of the liberty which Jesus purchased by taking upon Him the form of a slave and becoming obedient to death.

Acts 10:38
Isaiah 61:1

Philippians 2:7, 8
1 John 2:27
Psalm 133:2

2. "Because of the anointing" which we "have received of Him," because the precious ointment upon our High Priest's head goes down to the skirts of His garments, shared by His least and lowest members.

Perhaps we stop here and say, "But I cannot realize that I have received it, because my yoke is heavy upon me." Then see *how* you shall receive it; there is only one way—not by fresh revelation or special voice from heaven, but simply by faith—"that ye might receive the promise of the Spirit *through faith*." Give glory to God, and be fully persuaded that what He has promised He is able also to perform; and His "free Spirit" will be faithful to His promise, and the yoke, even *your* yoke, "shall be destroyed because of the anointing."

Galatians 3:14
Romans 4:20, 21

Psalm 51:12
Hebrews 10:23

All other yokes are sub-included in the yoke of our sins, and this is exactly what Jesus came to save us from; the very first, as it is the all-inclusive New Testament promise, "Thou shalt call His name Jesus: for He shall save His people from their sins." Are all His wonderful promises about this mere empty words, with no power or reality in them? Are they the exceptions to His declaration that "My words shall not pass away"? the only promises which are *not* Yea and Amen in Christ Jesus? Listen! they need no note or comment. "Sin shall not have dominion over you." "Ye were the servants of sin, but, ... being made free from sin, ye became the servants of righteousness." "*Now* being made free from sin," "the law of the Spirit of life in Christ Jesus hath made me free from the law of sin and death." "Whosoever committeth sin is the servant of sin ... If the Son therefore shall make you free, ye shall be free indeed." Let us look at the context of each (only not quoted for want of space), and, if our experience has nothing answering to all this purpose of His goodness, let us ask Him to show us His own meaning and His own royal intention, and to "reveal even this unto you" by the unction from the Holy One, who convinces all the more deeply of sin when He convinces also of the practical power of Christ's blood to cleanse from all sin, and of the reality of His present salvation. Do not hug the yoke which He has promised to destroy.

"And it shall come to pass in the day that the Lord shall give thee rest from thy sorrow, and from thy fear, and from the hard bondage wherein thou wast made to serve, that thou shalt ... say, How hath the oppressor ceased!" "In that day ... his burden shall be taken away from off thy shoulder." But "that day" may be *this* day! Why not? "For *now* will I break his yoke from off thee." "Where the Spirit of the Lord is, there is liberty"; and He hath said, "Ask, and ye *shall* receive." Recognise the anointing by faith, and then "stand fast therefore in the liberty wherewith Christ *hath* made us free, and be not entangled again with the yoke of bondage"; for "this is His commandment." Then you shall "walk at liberty," and give Him the glad "offering of a free

Matthew 1:21

Matthew 24:35
2 Cor. 1:20

Romans 6:14
Romans 6:17, 18
Romans 6:22
Romans 8:2
John 8:34, 36

Ephesians 1:4

Philippians 3:15
1 John 2:20
John 16:8
1 John 1:7
Matthew 1:21

Isaiah 14:3, 4

Isaiah 10:27

Nahum 1:13
2 Cor. 3:17
Matthew 7:7

Galatians 5:1

Psalm 119:45
Ps. 54:6, P.B.V.

Matthew 11:29
Jeremiah 34:15

heart," rejoicing in His easy yoke, and (shall we not add), "proclaiming liberty every man to his neighbour."

Upon Thy promises I stand,
Trusting in Thee: Thine own right hand
Doth keep and comfort me!
My soul doth triumph in Thy word;
Thine, Thine be all the praise, dear Lord,
As Thine the victory.

Love perfecteth what it begins;
Thy power doth save me from my sins;
Thy grace upholdeth me.
This life of trust, how glad! how sweet!
My need and Thy great fulness meet,
And I have all in Thee.

JEAN S. PIGOTT.

EIGHTEENTH DAY.

Our Works in God's Hand.

"Commit thy works unto the Lord."—Proverbs 16:3.

Psalm 103:20

SUPPOSE an angel were sent down to tell us this morning that he was commissioned to take all our work under his charge to-day, that we might just be easy about it, because he would undertake it, and his excellent strength and wisdom would make it all prosper a great deal more than ours, how extremely foolish it would be not to avail ourselves of such superhuman help! What a holiday it would seem, if we accepted the offer, as we went about our business with the angel beside us! what a day of privilege and progress! and how we should thank God for the extraordinary relief His kindness had sent!

Far higher is our privilege this day; not merely permitted, but pressed upon us by royal commandment, "Commit thy works unto Jehovah!" Yet this is but the third strand of a golden cord which is strong enough (if yielded to) to draw us up out of all the miry clay of the "pit of noise," where the voices of fear and anxiety and distrust make such a weary din. We are to commit the keeping of our souls to Him; then we shall be ready for the command to commit our way unto Him, and then our works. Then, having obeyed, we may exchange the less confident expression, "Unto God would I commit my cause," for the bright assurance, "I am persuaded that He is able to keep that which I *have* committed unto Him." *Of course* He is!

Psalm 40:2, margin

1 Peter 4:19
Psalm 37:5

Job 5:8
2 Timothy 1:12

Not an angel, but Jehovah bids us this day commit our works to Him. It is not approving the idea, nor thinking about it, nor even asking Him to take them, that is here commanded, but *committing* them: a definite act of soul, a real transaction with our Lord. Suppose you have an inter-

Psalm 55:22

view with another worker, and, having had a distinct under-standing as to what you wish him to undertake for you, you verbally and explicitly transfer to him the management and responsibility of some work. You are not actually in sight of it, you have no tangible objects to hand over, you might do it in a dark room, but the transaction is real. The burden of the work is no longer upon you, if only you have confidence in the one to whom you have committed it. And if you have the further confidence that he is considerably more ca-pable than yourself, and can do it all a great deal better, you are not only relieved but rejoiced. Just such a definite trans-

1 Peter 5:7

action does our Lord bid us make with Him this morning. Will you do it? Will you not, before venturing away from your quiet early hour, "commit thy works" to Him definite-ly, the special things you have to do to-day, and the unfore-seen work which He may add in the course of it?

And then, leave it with Him! You would not have the bad taste to keep on fidgeting about it to the friend who had kindly undertaken your work for you! If we would only apply the commonest rules of human courtesy and confi-dence to our intercourse with our Divine Master! Leave details and results all and altogether with Him. You see,

Eccles. 9:1

when you have committed it to Him, your "works *are* in the hand of God." Really in His hand! and where else would you wish them to be? Would you like to have them back in

Isaiah 40:12

your own? Do you think His grasp is not firm enough, or the hollow of His hand not large enough, to hold your lit-tle bits of work quite securely? Even if He tries your faith a little, and you seem to have laboured in vain and spent your strength for nought, cannot you trust your "own Master"

Isaiah 49:4
Isaiah 49:3

enough to add, "Yet *surely* my judgment is with the Lord, and my work with my God"? Especially as He says, "Thou art my servant, in whom I *will* be glorified"; by which "ye

1 Cor. 15:58
Isaiah 61:8

know that your labour is not in vain in the Lord."

That for the past work. For the present, "I will direct their work in truth." And for all our future work, a singular

Isaiah 65:22

shining in the eastern horizon: "Mine elect shall long enjoy the work of their hands."

Oh to be nothing, nothing!
  Only to lie at His feet,
A broken and emptied vessel,
  For the Master's use made meet.
Emptied, that He may fill me,
  As forth to His service I go;
Broken, that so unhindered
  His life through me might flow.

Oh to be nothing, nothing!
  Only as led by His hand;
A messenger at His gateway,
  Only waiting for His command.
Only an instrument ready
  His praises to sound at His will;
Willing, should He not require me,
  In silence to wait on Him still.

G. M. Taylor.

NINETEENTH DAY.

The Secret of Fulfilled Desire.

"Delight thyself also in the Lord and He shall give thee the desires of thy heart."—Psalm 37:4.

Proverbs 10:24
Matthew 19:6
Mark 10:35

James 4:2;
Proverbs 13:12

Psalm 73:25
Psalm 38:9
Isaiah 26:8, 9;
2 Samuel 23:5
Romans 12:2
Daniel 4:35

Romans 10:1;
Romans 11:26, 27

Ephesians 5:17

Psalm 37:3

ONE often hears this promise quoted without its conditional precept; but we have no right to put asunder anything that God has joined together. Every heart has desires, but not even every Christian heart delights itself in the Lord. This is the reason of the great wail of unfulfilled desire—the very howl, one might say, which makes a howling wilderness of this fair world.

It stands to reason; if our delight is absolutely and entirely in the Lord, all our desires will be not only "before Him," but the whole "desire of our soul" will be concentrated upon Him, radiating from that centre along the bright rays of His "good and perfect and acceptable will." Now, of course, His will must and will be carried out; for "He doeth according to His will in the army of heaven, and among the inhabitants of the earth: and none can stay His hand."

So, if we delight truly in the Lord, and thereby have our desires so harmonized with His will that they float out on the same great tide of perfect music, there will be no damper upon their vibrations, but they will be fulfilled for us because His will is fulfilled.

His will is not, as we are tempted practically to think, something quite separate and apart from Himself, so that we may think Him gracious, and yet think His will rather stern; or so that we may love Him, and yet very much dislike His will. His will is the very essence of Himself going forth in force; it is the primary difference between what we know of Jehovah and what the Hindoo imagines of Brahma.

We must not overlook the important word "also." This points us to a preliminary condition: "Trust in the Lord,

Isaiah 12:2, 3

and do good." Trust, evidenced by obedience, is the step-ping-stone to delight in the Lord, and the only one. Obedi-ence is the result of trust, and the condition of delight.

Two great cases of this condition of delight are distinctly given us—one spiritual, the other practical.

Job 22:23, 26

1. "If thou return to the Almighty, ... *then* thou shalt have thy delight in the Almighty." It is not said to saints, but

Matthew 9:11, 13
Luke 15:2, 32
Isaiah 44:22
Hosea 14:4

to repentant sinners—not to the eldest son, but to the re-turning prodigal. To me, the wanderer, it is offered. To me, the backslider, it is held out. We can never say: "The Lord does not mean such a one as I to delight in Him; that sort of thing is only meant for those who have always been con-sistent Christians." If so, He would not have said, "If thou

Job 22:23

return." Without true returning, there cannot be delight in the Lord; but, conversely, if there is no delight, ought we

Haggai 1:7

not to "consider our ways," lest some "returning" should be needed?

Isaiah 58:13, 14

2. "If thou turn away thy foot from the Sabbath, from doing thy pleasure on My holy day; and call the Sabbath a delight, the holy of the Lord, honourable; and shalt hon-our Him, not doing thine own ways, nor finding thine own pleasure, nor speaking thine own words: *Then* shalt thou de-light thyself in the Lord." On our knees before Him let us examine ourselves as to every clause of this great condition.

1 Kings 22:34
Micah 6:2
Job 15:11

Perhaps *here* we shall find the joints in the harness, the se-cret controversy which hinders the realization of delight in the Lord, and therefore of the annexed promise.

A word about the delight itself. There is something so real, and natural, and childlike about it. It is joy realized—joy in flower, bright, growing, alive, beautiful. It is the spar-kle of the up-springing fountain in the clear sunlight. This childlike delight is to be in the Lord Himself. It is quite an-other thing to delight in what He does for us. The Israelites

Neh. 9:25, 26

"delighted themselves in Thy great goodness. Nevertheless they were disobedient, and rebelled." Not under the shadow

Jonah 4:6
Song. 2:3
Psalm 40:8; 94:19;
119:47; 16:3

of even a God-given gourd, but under His own shadow, may you sit down "with great delight." Then all His fruits shall be sweet to your taste; you shall delight in His will, in His comforts, in His commandments, and in His people. You

Job 23:13   shall desire "what *His* soul desireth," and "He shall give thee
Psalm 145:19   the desires of thine heart."

> Oh, blessèd life!—the heart at rest
>   When all without tumultuous seems—
>   That trusts a higher will, and deems
> That higher will, not mine, the best.
>
> Oh, blessèd life!—heart, mind, and soul,
>   From self-born aims and wishes free,
>   In all at one with Deity,
> And loyal to the Lord's control.

W. T. MATSON.

TWENTIETH DAY.

Taking God at His Word.

"I believe God, that it shall be even as it was told me."—Acts 27:25.

Acts 27:22
Acts 27:37
Acts 27:18
Acts 27:20, 27
Acts 27:10
Acts 27:21

THEN, of course, St. Paul could be calm, and bright, and confident, "with a heart at leisure from itself" to cheer and counsel others. Yet could any circumstances have been more depressing?—a miserable and crowded ship, to which our most wretched steamer would be a palace, exceedingly tossed with tempest, not a gleam of sun or star for many days, all reckoning lost, driving wildly on to certain shipwreck, and the graphic and suggestive touch of "long abstinence."

Proverbs 27:1

Whatever this day may bring forth, there can be nothing like this for us. Yet even the lesser trials of our own journey may and must be met with the same simple and sufficient secret of calm, simple belief in what God has said.

Proverbs 16:3

It is strange and surprising even to ourselves how absolutely *enough* we always do find it, just to believe that it shall be

2 Chron. 32:8

even as God has told us, and "rest" on His word. The "it" may be for us one thing to-day, another tomorrow, according to the circumstances He sends; but the "shall be" cannot be severed from it. He has "told us" so much, that we have only to recognise our special need, to find at once that He has already "told" us exactly what we want.

Matthew 24:35

1 Peter 5:8

Glance at the needs of this day—our weakness, our openness to temptation, our liability to fall, our besetting sins, our ignorance, our present or possible troubles, our longing for Himself, which includes all other holy longing—seven pressing realities. Now let us hush our hearts to listen to the reality of His corresponding replies: "I will strengthen thee." "Ye shall be able to quench *all* the fiery darts of the wicked." "Able to keep you from falling" (*Gr.*

Ps. 73:22; 60:11
Psalm 63:1

Isaiah 41:10
Ephesians 6:16
Jude 24

Matthew 1:21
Psalm 32:8
John 14:18

"stumbling"). "He shall save His people from *their* sins" (*i.e.* just your own special ones). "I will instruct thee and teach thee in the way which thou shalt go." "I will not leave you comfortless." "I will come to you." Can we read these words—His own words, and say, "I do *not* believe God!" Even the recoil from such an expression may help a trembling one to the joyful and only alternative: "I believe God, that it shall be *even as* it was told me." Not less, not almost as, but "even as," with God's own fulness of meaning in each word of each promise.

1 Chron. 17:23–25

David prayed: "Do as Thou hast said ... For Thou, O my God, hast *told* Thy servant that Thou wilt build him an house: *therefore* Thy servant hath found in his heart to pray before Thee." And because God had "promised this good-

1 Chron. 17:26, 27

ness," he prayed on confidently: "Now *therefore* let it please Thee to bless ... : for Thou blessest, O Lord, and it shall be blessed for ever." Has He not "told" us of blessings be-

Ephesians 1:3

yond those for which David pleaded, and may we not claim these in the name of Jesus with a childlike, "Do as Thou hast said"?

The ground of St. Paul's belief was not something, but Some One. Simply, "I believe *God*"! An earnest worker said the other day, "Oh, I am so glad it does not say, 'I know

2 Timothy 1:12

what I have believed,' but, 'I know *whom* I have believed'!" This belief, of course, includes all His messages, written or

Isaiah 7:9

spoken. "If ye will not believe, surely ye shall not be established," is a word of continual application to the trem-

1 John 3:23
2 Chron. 20:20

bling or wavering steps of our daily path. But "this is His commandment," "Believe in the Lord your God, so shall ye be established; believe His prophets, so shall ye prosper."

Luke 1:45

And then, "Blessed is she that believed: for there shall be a performance of those things which were *told* her from the Lord."

Acts 27:25, 44

"Even *as* it was told me." "And *so* it came to pass."

TWENTY-FIRST DAY.

Our Commission.

"And let him that heareth say, Come."—Revelation 22:17.

Ezra 8:36

" THEY delivered the king's commissions unto the king's lieutenants." Have some of us thought it would be easier to work for God if a definite commission were delivered to us, so that we could know exactly what we were to do and say?—a commission so explicit, that there could be no mistake either in its personal delivery to ourselves or in our execution of it? Then here it is!

Joshua 1:16

To whom is it delivered? Simply to "him that heareth." "The Spirit and the bride say, Come. And let him that heareth say, Come." Then, if this blessed call has been heard by you, for you is the commission intended, and to you it is given. Not, are you a fit and polished instrument? not, are you a practised worker? not, are you already a trained soldier, and therefore very capable of enlisting others? not, have you a special gift of speech or pen? but simply and solely, have you heard for yourself the one sweet call, "Come"?

Revelation 22:17

Isaiah 49:2
2 Timothy 2:2, 3

1 Cor. 12:7–11
Matthew 11:28

Now you see that the commission is for you, do you not? But what is it? Can anything be more simple and explicit? You are to "say, *Come*"! That is all; but, in simple obedience to this command of your King, what possibilities of blessing and success, of gladness to you and glory to Him, are enfolded! You are to "*say*, Come." Are you saying it? Not, are you exercising a general good influence? not, do you try to lead and keep the conversation in profitable channels? not, do you speak about "good things" or even *about* Christ? not, are you giving time and money to the furtherance of some branch of His work?—you may be doing all this, and yet be distinctly disobeying His command, distinctly faithless and disobedient to your commission.

Acts 4:20, 31

Jeremiah 23:28

Luke 16:10

Proverbs 11:30	You are missing the present privilege and unspeakable hap-
Daniel 12:3	piness of winning souls, and foregoing the glorious reward
	annexed to it. For, assuredly, it is those who are literally say-
John 4:29, 30, 39	ing "Come," who are really "turning many to righteous-

You are missing the present privilege and unspeakable happiness of winning souls, and foregoing the glorious reward annexed to it. For, assuredly, it is those who are literally saying "Come," who are really "turning many to righteousness"; not because they are more gifted, but because God's powerful blessing is given with their obedience to His definite command.

Why should we be at a loss what to say, when He has given us the very word? We have but to transmit the echo of His own call, "Come unto Me"; "Come and see"; "If any man thirsts let him come unto Me and drink."

Whatever the position of the one to whom we speak, there is always a suitable "Come." "Come thou with us, and we will do thee good." "Come and see Him whom we have found." "Come and let us join ourselves to the Lord in a perpetual covenant that shall not be forgotten." Then, for those who have come, there is still always a "Come up higher." "Come up with me … that we may fight against the Canaanite." "Come ye, and let us walk in the light of the Lord." Oh, how such a call may be blessed to a weak-handed and feeble-footed Christian! And still there is a "come" of special beauty and power for those who have yielded themselves to Him: "Now ye have consecrated yourselves unto the Lord, come *near*." And let us not shrink from faithfully echoing with no "uncertain sound," "Come *out* from among them," remembering that when the heavenly Bridegroom says, "Come *with* Me," He adds, "*from* Lebanon … *from* the lions' dens." He who gives the commission *always* gives opportunities of exercising it; but it is our part faithfully to seek and watch for these, and courage and faith will increase as they widen. The servant who was sent at first only to *say* "Come" to the bidden guests, was next sent to *bring* them in from a wider range, and then to "*compel* them to come in" from a wider still.

The commission is laid before you this day; it is inscribed with your own name, signed by your King's own hand, and sealed by the Spirit, who bears witness with your spirit that His "Come" has been heard by you. Do you accept it? or do you refuse it? There is no third alternative!

Side references:
- John 1:39, 46
- John 7:37
- Numbers 10:29
- John 1:46
- Jeremiah 50:5
- Proverbs 25:7
- Judges 1:3
- Isaiah 2:5
- Hebrews 12:12
- 2 Chron. 29:31
- 1 Cor. 14:8
- 2 Cor. 6:17
- Song. 4:8
- Acts 1:8
- Luke 14:17, 21
- Luke 14:23
- Hebrews 3:13
- Romans 8:16

Ye who hear the blessèd call
    Of the Spirit and the Bride,
Hear the Master's word to all,
    Your commission and your guide:
"And let him that heareth say,
Come," to all yet far away.

"Come!" alike to age and youth;
    Tell them of our Friend above,
Of His beauty and His truth,
    Preciousness, and grace, and love.
Tell them what you know is true,
Tell them what He is to you.

Brothers, sisters, do not wait,
    Speak for Him who speaks to you!
Wherefore should you hesitate?
    This is no great thing to do.
Jesus only bids you say,
"Come!" and will you not obey?

TWENTY-SECOND DAY.

Beholding and Declaring.

"Son of man, behold with thine eyes, and hear with thine ears, and set thine heart upon all that I shall shew thee; for to the intent that I might shew them unto thee art thou brought hither: declare all that thou seest to the house of Israel."—Ezekiel 40:4.

Ezekiel 40:3
Matthew 21:27

John 14:26
John 16:15
1 Cor. 2:9

1 Cor. 2:10
Ezekiel 40, etc.

1 Cor. 2:9

Isaiah 64:4
Ezekiel 43:1, 2, 6

2 Cor. 3:18
John 10:3

Song. 3:11

Isaiah 55:3

WHETHER the mysterious Measurer was a created angel or the divine Angel of the Covenant, "we cannot tell." But the message which he here gives to Eze-kiel seems to illustrate the work of the Holy Spirit, whose of-fice it is to take both the words and the things of Christ and shew them unto us.

"Eye hath not seen," yet "behold with thine eyes"; "nor ear heard," yet "hear with thine ears"; "neither have entered into the heart of man," yet set thine heart upon all that I shall show thee." For "God hath revealed them unto us by His Spirit." To Ezekiel should be shown the wonder-ful temple, with its measurements, its laws, and its mystical services. To us shall be revealed the things which God hath prepared for them that love Him, and (as if to let the ladder down a step lower) "for him that waiteth for Him." After-ward, he [Ezekiel] beheld "the glory of the God of Israel," and "he heard Him speaking unto" him. And we, by the Spirit, are to behold the glory of the Lord, and to "hear his voice" calling us by name.

This would seem to be all promise and privilege, rather than commandment; something with which we have noth-ing at all to do but to wait and see if it comes! Nay! "Be-hold with thine eyes." "Go forth and behold" your King! And when we accept the seemingly impossible command, the Spirit will open our eyes that we may see. "Hear with thine ears!" And with (not even after) the obedient incli-nation of the ear, the still small voice will outring not only

John 10:16
Isaiah 52:6
Isaiah 35:5

Colossians 3:2

John 16:15
Psalm 17:7; 103:7;
25:14; Exodus 33:
18, 19; Dan. 11:2
Jeremiah 33:3
John 16:13

Ezekiel 40:2

Acts 10:19

Acts 4:20; 1 Jn 1:3
Ezekiel 43:10
Luke 2:17

Isa. 6:5; Ps. 96:10,
P.B.V.; Ezek. 3:10,
11; Matt. 10:27

2 Cor. 4:13

"earth's drowsy chime," but all other voices. He says: "They shall hear My voice"; "they shall know in that day that I am He that doth speak." For the Spirit will unstop the ears of the deaf. When He thus makes us behold and hear, He will finish the work and enable us to "set" our wandering hearts upon all that He will show us. But the responsibility will still be ours to follow the enabling.

It will act and react. The more we set our hearts, the more He will show us; and the more He shows us, the more our hearts will surely there be fixed.

"*All* that I shall shew thee." What a vista of revelation opens before us! "He shall take of Mine and shall shew it unto you,"—My love, My grace, My wisdom, My acts, My covenant, My goodness, My glory! He "will shew thee the truth." He "will shew thee great and mighty things, which thou knowest not," "He will shew you things to come." Do we not feel like little children, wondering, in delighted expectation, what it is that we are going to see?

Like little children, too, we have been brought hither, on purpose that He may show us all this. "Hither," to the very place, the very point, where we now are. We did not come of ourselves; we were "brought." Very likely we should have gone to some other place, and aimed at some other point. But He brought us hither, with gracious intent of revelation. It may have been a stiff climb up the "very high mountain"; but who minds that, if they really believe in the promised view?

As commands always lead up to privileges, so privileges again lead on to further commands. Not for ourselves alone are we to "see" and "hear." We are to declare all that we see. When we have seen the house, we are to "shew the house." When we have seen the Saviour, we are to make known abroad the saying which was told us concerning Him. When we have seen the King, we are to "tell it out" that He reigneth. "Hear with thine ears, and go ... and speak." "What I tell you in darkness, that speak ye in light."

Do not let us begin quibbling about how much we can tell, or how much we ought to tell. Let us very simply and very humbly bow before this "His commandment," and ask

Him to enable us to obey it exactly as He means us to obey it, neither losing the spirit in the letter nor ignoring the letter in the spirit.

> Lord, speak to me, that I may speak
> > In living echoes of Thy tone;
> As Thou hast sought, so let me seek
> > Thy erring children, lost and lone.
>
> Oh teach me, Lord, that I may teach
> > The precious things Thou dost impart;
> And wing my words, that they may reach
> > The hidden depths of many a heart.
>
> Oh fill me with Thy fulness, Lord,
> > Until my very heart o'erflow,
> In kindling thought and glowing word,
> > Thy love to tell, Thy praise to show.

TWENTY-THIRD DAY.

Telling of the Hand of God.

"Then I told them of the hand of my God which was good upon me; as also the king's words that he had spoken unto me. And they said, Let us rise up and build. So they strengthened their hands for this good work."—Nehemiah 2:18.

Malachi 3:16

" THEN they that feared the Lord spake often one to another." Yet many hold back from what they call "talking about religion," under colour that they fear it too often leads to talking about self. And yet, what about the general conversation which is about "other things," not "the things which are Jesus Christ's"? Are the "other things" free from self, and wholly profitable? Is it "with grace, seasoned with salt"? Yet this is what we are commanded that our speech should "*always*" be.

Mark 4:19
Philippians 2:21
Job 15:3;
Colossians 4:6

Let us lay aside this unscriptural notion of "talking about religion," which may only be controversy and criticism, and see what our Lord would have us talk about. The sum of our conversation should be, as recorded of Anna, "She ... spake of Him." Here is our keynote, and what wealth of melody and fulness of harmony spring from it!—the melodies of His word "in linked sweetness, long drawn out," for the right hand; the harmonies of His works, in ever-varying marvels, for the left. Why, we have topics for all eternity, much more for our occasional hours and minutes of converse, unfolding more and more as we receive more and more of His fulness!

Luke 2:38

Deut. 6:7
Colossians 3:16
Psalm 105:2, 5
Psalm 9:1

John 1:16

But there is the point. If we do not want to "speak of Him," let us beware of plausibly persuading ourselves that it is because we do not want to speak about ourselves. Let us be honest, and own that the vessel does not overflow because it is not very full of faith and love. Christ said, "Out of the abundance of the heart the mouth speaketh." Men

Eccles. 11:3
Matthew 12:34

say, "No such thing! one does not speak when one's heart is full!" Yet "let God be true, but every man a liar," and let us see whether our unwillingness to speak of Him does not arise from our having nothing to say.

Nehemiah had something to tell. "I told them of the hand of my God which was good upon me." Nothing about his "own arm," but "Thy right hand and Thine arm," and what that had done, the wonderful answer to his prayer, and the way made plain before his face. And see how it stirred up his listeners forthwith! They said, "Let us rise up and build. So they strengthened their hands for this good work." Have we nothing to tell to those whom we meet this day of what the hand of our God has done?

David said, "Come and hear, ... and I will declare what He hath done for my soul"; and no doubt then, as now, the story of His gracious doings resulted in stimulus and blessing to other souls. When thus "confession with the mouth is made," it is very, very often "unto salvation" for the listeners.

We must first know and "consider how great things He hath done for" us; and then the voice of Jesus says not only "*Shew*," but "*Tell* how great things the Lord hath done for thee," that thus showing, and thus telling, "the communication of thy faith may become *effectual* by the acknowledging of every good thing which is in you in Christ Jesus."

We have also less personal but not less vivid testimony to bear. "The Lord hath done great things for us, whereof we are glad," will put a new song in many another's mouth, and confirm their faith in the living God. Thus did Moses, and the result was not only that Jethro rejoiced for all the goodness which the Lord had done, but that he rose to the grand confession, "*Now I know* that Jehovah is greater than all gods."

It is not to be only a one-sided telling, but a free and pleasant interchange; for we are distinctly commanded, "*Talk* ye of all His wondrous works." Who can exhaust that "*all*"! While we "talk together of all these things," communing together like the disciples on the Emmaus road, how often does Jesus Himself draw near and go with us! I

Romans 3:4

Nehemiah 2:18

Psalm 44:3
Neh. 1:10; 2:4, 8

Nehemiah 2:18

Psalm 77:12

Psalm 66:16

Romans 10:10

1 Samuel 12:24

Mark 5:19;
Luke 8:39
Philemon 6

Isaiah 63:7
Psalm 126:3
Psalm 40:3
Exodus 18:8, 9

Exodus 18:11

Psalm 105:2
Psalm 77:12
Luke 24:14
Luke 24:15

Luke 24:31

Psalm 19:11
Psalm 119:27

think He *always* does, only our eyes are not always open to recognise Him.   Verily, in keeping of this commandment (and it *is* a commandment), " there is *great* reward."

" Make me to understand the way of Thy precepts : so shall I talk of Thy wondrous works."

Have you not a word for Jesus? not a word to say for
    Him?
He is listening through the chorus of the burning
    seraphim!
He is listening; does He hear you speaking of the
    things of earth,
Only of its passing pleasure, selfish sorrow, empty
    mirth?
He has spoken words of blessing, pardon, peace, and
    love to you,
Glorious hopes and gracious comfort, strong and
    tender, sweet and true;
Does He hear you telling others something of His
    love untold,
Overflowings of thanksgiving for His mercies
    manifold?

TWENTY-FOURTH DAY.

————

Telling of the King's Words.

"Then I told them of … the king's words that he had spoken unto me. And they said, Let us rise up and build. So they strengthened their hands for this good work." — Nehemiah 2:18.

HOW naturally we should not only treasure, but *tell,* any royal words spoken to ourselves! They would be more to us than any other utterances, and they would ensure the interest of our listeners. How natural for Nehemiah to tell of the king's words which he had spoken unto him, though only an earthly and alien sovereign!

Now, ought it not to be just as natural, delightful, and interesting to tell of the words of our own, our heavenly King, especially when He has commanded, "He that hath My word, let him speak My word faithfully"? Not that we can ever tell all that passes in the secret audience chamber; nor would it be well that we should try to do so: for "the secret of the Lord is with them that fear Him." The King has gifts for us with shining inscriptions which "no man knoweth saving he that receiveth" them, whispers which cannot resound in words.

But very much, perhaps most, of His gracious communications to the soul come in the very form which is most easily grasped, remembered, and repeated—His own written words brought to our remembrance by His good Spirit, and applied to our conscious or unconscious need. Do not let us give our own memories the credit, instead of giving Him the praise, when He so kindly sends any of His own words freshly and forcibly into our minds. Have we not often defrauded Him of the glory due unto His name in this matter, by mistaking His voice for our mere observation or recollection?

Jeremiah 23:28

Mark 4:34

Psalm 25:14
Revelation 2:17;
Proverbs 17:8

John 14:26
Acts 20:35

Psalm 29:2

Hosea 2:14, margin; Mark 4:10,11
Haggai 1:13

Ezekiel 3:10

Ezekiel 2:2
Deut. 6:6
Deut. 6:7

Habakkuk 2:1

Daniel 10:19
Daniel 10:21

Micah 2:7;
Isaiah 55:10, 11;
Jeremiah 23:29
Jeremiah 23:28
Mark 8:38

John 6:63
Isaiah 55:11
1 Peter 1:23; 2:2

Matthew 25:16

2 Timothy 2:2

Now it is these words of the King, spoken to our hearts as they are not spoken to the world, which we may profitably tell others, thus becoming "the Lord's messenger in the Lord's message," and spreading the knowledge of His words. Nehemiah did not tell of the king's words which he had spoken unto somebody else, but "which he had *spoken unto me.*" So, if we would tell the King's words, we must first hear them. Ask that, like Ezekiel, the Spirit may enter into us when He speaks unto us, so that we may hear Him that speaks unto us. "These words shall be in thine heart"; and then, after that, comes the command: "Talk of them when thou sittest in thine house, and when thou walkest by the way."

Watch to see what He will say, and no fear but that His words will be heard, and that more and more. For it is when He *hath* spoken unto us that we shall be strengthened, and say, "Let my Lord speak." And then He will say more to us, and show us "that which is noted in the Scripture of truth."

It seems a truism to say that this telling of the King's words will be ever so much more useful and resultful than our own words. Yet do we always act upon this? When we try to "speak a word for Jesus" to a friend, does it not sometimes seem as if we were a little "ashamed of His words"? Is there not sometimes a little shrinking from giving a text? Has it not seemed an easier course to talk about a sermon? If we have visited a cottage, have we not sometimes thought our duty discharged by a little general good advice and kindly sympathy, and not *always* "told them of the King's words," which are spirit and life, and which should not have returned void—seed words, by which dead souls might have been born again; "sincere milk," by which babes in Christ might "grow"?

Surely there is no more precious talent entrusted to us, none with which we may trade with more certain success and splendid increase, than these words of our King. What we hear from Him let us commit to others, "that they may be able to teach others also." A simple text thus passed on (and who cannot do this!) may be the immediate means of

Psalm 119:50

2 Cor. 1:4

wonderful spiritual help and quickening, and "*the* comfort wherewith we ourselves are comforted of God" (not some otherwise concocted comfort) may comfort many "which are in any trouble," without even one word of man as its vehicle.

> Yes, we have a word for Jesus! Living echoes we will be
> Of Thine own sweet words of blessing, of Thy gracious "Come to Me."
> Jesus, Master! yes, we love Thee, and to prove our love would lay
> Fruit of lips which Thou wilt open, at Thy blessèd feet to-day.
> Many an effort it may cost us, many a heart-beat, many a fear,
> But Thou knowest, and wilt strengthen, and Thy help is always near.
> Give us grace to follow fully, vanquishing our faithless shame,
> Feebly it may be, but truly, witnessing for Thy dear name.

TWENTY-FIFTH DAY.

Evil Speaking.

"Speak not evil one of another, brethren."—James 4:11.

Deut. 10:13

2 Cor. 12:9
Philippians 4:19
Titus 3:2

Psalm 119:96

Titus 3:2

1 Peter 2:1

Ephesians 4:31

Hebrews 12:15

James 2:8
Zech. 7:10; 8:17
1 Cor. 13:1
1 Cor. 13:2, 5

Philippians 4:8

ONE of the most difficult of "His commandments," and yet one which is in a peculiar degree "for our good" and personal happiness, as well as for those around us! The more difficult, the more need of grace; and the more need, the more the full supply.

Well might St. Paul say, "Put them in mind to speak evil of no man," for do we not easily fail to keep this in mind? The command is "exceeding broad"; let us not seek to narrow it, but humbly bow to our Master's distinct orders in all their exactness.

Do we really *wish* to know them fully, that we may obey fully? Then what are they? "Speak evil of *no* man." Shall we venture practically to say, "Yes, Lord, *except* of So-and-so"?

"Laying aside *all* evil speakings." Does not this include the very least?

"Let *all* bitterness, ... and evil speaking, be put away from you"; then does He give us leave to cherish even one little hidden root of that bitterness from which the evil speaking springs?

"Put away" implies resolute action in the matter,—have we even *tried* to "put away *all*"?

But this great clause of the "royal law" is broader still: "Let none of you *imagine* evil in your hearts against his neighbour." And the characteristic of that charity, without which we are only "sounding brass" and "nothing," is, that it *"thinketh"* no evil. Is not this the root from which the far-poisoning fruit springs? We have first disobeyed another order: "Whatsoever things are of good report; ... think on *these* things." Instead of that, we "think" about the bad reports that we may have heard; we develop the unkind hint into suspicion, and perhaps into accusation, by *thinking* about it, instead of thinking on and thinking out the probable "other side" of the case. This thinking has tempted us

1 Peter 3:10

not to "refrain our tongue"; and thus we have set some one else "thinking," and thereby to more speaking evil one of

James 3:5

another. At last the little fire has kindled a great matter, and we come ourselves and bring others under the condemna-

Psalm 15:3

tion of taking up "a reproach against his neighbour," instead of not enduring nor receiving it (see the striking marginal reading). And what is the just penalty annexed by impli-

Psalm 15:1

cation? *Not* to abide in His tabernacle, *not* to dwell in His holy hill!

2 Peter 2:12
Jude 10

How very often we speak evil of things which we, more or less, "understand not"—ah, even of "things which they *know* not"!—instead of obeying another part of the royal

1 Cor. 4:5

law, "Judge nothing before the time, until the Lord come," when the very person whom we have been condemning shall "have praise of God!" This often arises from disobedi-

Proverbs 25:9

ence to two other plain commands: "Debate thy cause with thy neighbour himself, and discover not a secret to anoth-

Matthew 18:15

er:" and, "Go and tell him his fault between thee and him *alone*." Yet away we go, and tell somebody else about it instead!

Let us guard against the negative form of evil speaking, generally the most dangerous and cruel, even when the most thoughtless. Absalom was extremely clever in this. Who

2 Samuel 15:3–5
2 Peter 2:10

could quote any actual evil speaking against his royal father? Who could charge him with speaking evil of dignities? And yet by insinuation, by his way of putting things, by his very manner, he wrought a thousand-fold more cruel harm than any amount of speaking out could possibly have done. Oh to be watchful as to such omissions to speak well, as amount to speaking evil! watchful as to the eloquence of even a hesitation, watchful as to the forcible language of feature and eye!

Of course the question arises: "But what about cases in which wrong-doing must be spoken of for the sake of truth and justice?" Clear as crystal are our instructions here:

Ephesians 4:15

Colossians 3:17
1 Cor. 10:31

Proverbs 4:23
Psalm 141:3

Job 15:3

1. We are to speak "the truth." *The* truth, not such part of it as will best prove our case, and nothing else! Not what we *suppose* to be the truth. 2. "In love." Does all our testimony stand *this* test? 3. "In the name of the Lord Jesus." Would not this check many a word against another? 4. "To the glory of God." Failure in any one of these four rules brings us in guilty of sin. Oh may He give us grace to keep our heart with all diligence, and Himself set a watch this day before our mouth, and keep the door of our lips! May we cease to "reason with unprofitable talk, or with speeches *wherewith we can do no good.*"

Take my lips, and let them be
Filled with messages from Thee.

TWENTY-SIXTH DAY.

Hindering.

"Lest we should hinder the gospel of Christ."—1 Corinthians 9:12.

MANY an active and willing helper in the Church is too often an unconscious hinderer of the gospel. Let us each try to find out how we may have hindered, that we may do so no more.

A vexation arises, and our expressions of impatience hinder others from taking it patiently. Disappointment, ailment, or even weather depresses us; and our look or tone of depression hinders others from maintaining a cheerful and thankful spirit. We let out a fearing or discouraged remark, and another's hope and zeal is wet-blanketed. "What man is there that is fearful and faint-hearted? let him go and return unto his house, lest his brethren's heart faint as well as his heart."

We *say* an unkind thing, and another is hindered in learning the holy lesson of charity that *thinketh* no evil. We say a provoking thing, and our sister or brother is hindered in that day's effort to be meek. "Make straight paths for *your* feet, lest that which is lame be turned out of the way."

We yield an inch in some doubtful matter, and another is emboldened to take an ell.[1] We do an inexpedient thing, and another improves upon the supposed example, and feels justified in doing an unlawful thing. "Abstain from all appearance of evil." "Let not your good be evil spoken of."

We miss an opportunity of speaking "a word for Jesus"; and our pleasant, commonplace talk has checked a half-formed wish for something better, and hindered the light of the glorious gospel from shining into a heart. We do not heed the thoughtful look on some household face just after family prayer or public worship, and our needless chat about

(marginal references)
Deut. 20:8
Judges 7:3

James 4:11
1 Cor. 13:5
James 1:26
Hebrews 12:13

1 Cor. 10:23
1 Cor. 8:13
1 Thess. 5:22
Romans 14:16
Colossians 4:6

2 Cor. 4:4

Philippians 3:19
Matthew 13:4

Isaiah 50:4
Psalm 119:130
Luke 11:52
Psalm 69:6

Psalm 69:6

1 Cor. 15:33
Proverbs 22:25;
1 Cor. 5:6

Numbers 32:7

John 15:22
Galatians 5:7

Genesis 24:56
1 Thess. 2:18

2 Cor. 4:10
2 Thess. 1:8
Hebrews 10:24

"earthly things" acts the fowls of the air. We make a critical remark about a preacher or writer, and it is brought back by the enemy in swift temptation, at the very moment when a word in season was about to find entrance. "Them that were entering in, ye hindered." Oh, terrible condemnation! "Let not those that seek Thee be confounded for *my* sake."

We need, too, to be shown whether we are quite unconsciously hindering in even lesser ways; for many have little peculiarities, of which they are hardly or not at all aware, which nevertheless annoy, fidget, depress, or chill those with whom they have much intercourse, and thus hinder the calm reign of peace in their spirits. "Let not them that wait on Thee, O Lord God of hosts, be ashamed for my sake."

How sadly, too, we may hinder without word or act! For wrong feeling is more infectious than wrongdoing; especially the various phases of ill-temper – gloominess, touchiness, discontent, irritability,—do we not know how catching these are? If the Lord asked us, "*Wherefore* discourage ye the heart of the children of Israel" in this way, should we not be utterly without excuse? What if He asked each hindered one, "*Who* did hinder you?"—are our consciences sure that our names would escape mention?

Shall we not watch and pray that this day we may only help and not hinder in the least thing, and that no one may have virtually to say to us, "Hinder me not"! May we never be the helpers of the great hinderer! When "Satan hindered" St. Paul, he probably found human agents.

Let us ask that the Lord Jesus would so perfectly tune our spirits to the keynote of His exceeding great love, that all our unconscious influence may breathe only of that love, and help all with whom we come in contact to obey the gospel of our Lord Jesus Christ. "And let us *consider* one another, to provoke unto love and to good works."

[1]An "ell" is an old measure of length, approximately 45 inches.

TWENTY-SEVENTH DAY.

Strengthening Hands.

"Strengthen ye the weak hands, and confirm the feeble knees."—Isaiah 35:3.

Luke 11:23

" **H**E that is not with Me is against Me: and he that gathereth not with Me scattereth." So it is not enough merely not to hinder; we must help: for not helping generally amounts to hindering. Perhaps we tried yesterday not to be hinderers; to-day let us "go on to completeness," and try to be helpers.

Heb. 6:1 (Gr.)

"Strengthen ye the weak hands." Plenty of these around us; for where is one real worker who does not feel his weakness, even in very proportion to what seems to us his strength? It does not the least follow that those who are altogether much stronger than ourselves are not perhaps realizing their weakness much more. We "should not think of such a thing" as aiming to strengthen their hands, and so very much mutual ministry is left undone. A little child may strengthen the hands of a giant and veteran in the faith, and it is just the giants and veterans who do *not* say to the more feeble members, "I have no need of you."

2 Cor. 12:10

1 Cor. 2:3

1 Chron. 19:12

1 Cor. 12:21, 22

2 Samuel 10:2
2 Cor. 7:6
Titus 1:4
2 Cor. 7:7

"David sent to comfort Hanun by the hand of his servants." St. Paul received the comfort of God by the coming of Titus, his "own son" in the faith; and he seems to have had a great deal of both comfort and joy (which certainly are most strengthening), at second hand, by the "fervent mind toward" him of the Corinthians, so that "exceedingly the more joyed we."

2 Cor. 7:13

Proverbs 3:27

Again, those very near us often need strengthening; are we right if they have practically to look farther for the strengthening which it might be ours to give? There may be a spiritual application of providing specially for those of our own house.

1 Timothy 5:8

Again, are there not sometimes such very "weak hands," that we almost get tired of trying to strengthen them, and feel inclined to think it is no use dealing with such hopeless feebleness? What if our Master did this to us?

How shall we set about it? First, by prayer, as Aaron and Hur held up the hands of Moses. "Helping together by prayer." This reaches all. Who knows how much of the weakness of hands, which distresses or even annoys us, may be laid at our door because we talked about it instead of praying about it? Very likely, names will occur to us now; then take those names at once to the Mighty One, and ask Him this morning to strengthen those weak hands and confirm those feeble knees.

Secondly, by personal contact. I suppose we never come in contact with one who is really strong in the Lord without being strengthened, whether we feel it or not. But we should not be content with the unconscious influence which it is our singular privilege to radiate. "Jonathan arose, and went to David in the wood, and strengthened his hand in God." Arising always implies a little effort. Then make it! What are our orders? "Comfort ye, comfort ye My people, saith your God." How are we to do it? "Speak ye *to the heart* of Jerusalem." What comes from the heart goes to the heart. "*Speak*"; don't hint and beat about the bush. When the arrow is feathered with love and weighted with wisdom, it must fly straight. What are we to say? "Say ... Be strong, fear not; behold, your God will come with vengeance, even God with a recompense; He will come and save you." "Cry unto her, that her warfare is accomplished, that her iniquity is pardoned." Examine these two wonderful messages, and see if they do not actually include everything required for your fulfilment of this commandment. You may amplify them, but that is all. Take with you His words, and then you may say without presumption, "I would strengthen you with my mouth."

Before we can really lift up other hands, our own must have been lifted up by His good Spirit, and our own feeble knees must have been confirmed by much bowing at His footstool. "When *thou* art converted, strengthen thy breth-

Romans 15:1

Exodus 17:12
2 Cor. 1:11

Proverbs 25:9

James 5:16

Ephesians 6:10

1 Samuel 23:16

Isaiah 40:1
Isaiah 40:2,
margin

Isaiah 35:4

Isaiah 40:2

Job 16:5

Hebrews 12:12, 13

Ephesians 3:13, 16
Luke 22:32

Psalm 51:12, 13

ren." "Uphold *me* with Thy free Spirit. *Then* will I teach." It is the climax of the grand procession of promises in that

Job 22:21–29

magnificent close of the words of Eliphaz. If we acquaint ourselves with God, receive His law, return to Him, and put away iniquity, *then* "when men are cast down, then thou shalt say, There is lifting up."

Job 4:3,4

May our record on high be: "Thou hast strengthened the weak hands. Thy words have upholden him that was falling, and thou hast strengthened the feeble knees."

> Oh lead me, Lord, that I may lead
>   The wandering and the wavering feet;
> Oh feed me, Lord, that I may feed
>   Thy hungering ones with manna sweet.
>
> Oh strengthen me, that while I stand
>   Firm on the Rock, and strong in Thee,
> I may stretch out a loving hand
>   To wrestlers with the troubled sea.

TWENTY-EIGHTH DAY.

Seeking to Excel.

"Seek that ye may excel."—1 Corinthians 14:12.

1 Cor. 1:2 · A N almost startling command; yet it is addressed to "*all* that in *every* place call upon the name of Jesus Christ our Lord," therefore unmistakably to ourselves.

Isaiah 55:8 · Very likely our thoughts have been quite different from God's thoughts about it. We have been thinking it was useless to seek to excel, because we saw no likelihood of doing so; that it was presumptuous to think of such a thing; that it was even positively wrong to aim at it; yet, all the time, there the commandment stood, "Seek that ye may excel!"

1 Cor. 14:12 · For its right fulfilment, there must be one preliminary and one object. The preliminary is, that we must be "zealous of spiritual gifts." It is only when we are coveting earnestly the best gifts that the exercise and development of all others comes in its right place; that is, we must be eagerly desiring and heartily striving and using His own means to grow in grace, to receive always more and more of His fulness, more light and love, more faith and power, more, above all, of His Spirit.

1 Cor. 12:31

1 Peter 2:2

2 Peter 3:18

John 1:16

1 Thess. 3:12

1 Thess. 4:1

2 Cor. 10:12 · Even when this is the case, how often we set some human standard before us, and say: "Ah! if I only had half as much grace as So-and-so!" Comparing ourselves among ourselves, we are not wise; it is a fruitful source of limitation and hindrance. We are not to aim at "half as much grace," nor even *as* much, but at *excelling* the fair self-chosen standard, which after all is so far below the "exceeding abundantly" which He is able to do for us. Let us give it up, once for all, and strike out into God's more excellent way, and "seek to excel." Let us open our mouth wide that He may fill it, asking for such great gifts that His royal bounty may

Ephesians 3:20

1 Cor. 12:31

Psalm 81:10

2 Cor. 9:11

Ephesians 1:19
2 Cor. 4:7
2 Thess. 1:11, 12

be magnified because of our very poverty; asking for such excellency of power that it may be *seen* to be of Him and not of us; asking that He would so fulfil *all* the good pleasure of His goodness, that the name of our Lord Jesus Christ may be glorified in us.

Jeremiah 45:5

Then, the one object. "Seekest thou great things for thyself? seek them not." But "seek that ye may excel *to the edifying of the Church*."

Galatians 5:20
James 3:16
1 Cor. 10:23

James 1:17

Apart from this, seeking to excel would inevitably become sin. Emulation, ambition, pride, would come in like a flood; envying and strife would follow, leading to "confusion and every evil work." "All things edify not,"—should not this guide the directions in which we seek to excel? For this end only let every good gift, spiritual or mental, inward or even outward, be continually cultivated and carefully used. Let us this day and henceforth aim at nothing lower.

Luke 16:10

Perhaps He grants us power to excel in some seemingly very little things, some little peculiar gifts which we don't think much of. "He that is faithful in that which is *least*," will be enabled to use even that for the edifying of some part of the Church. Those who have no hand in raising the strong pillars, may yet be called to give a delicate touch to the lily work which shall crown them. "To every man his work"; and in that, even if it is only running little errands for the skilled workmen, we may excel to the edifying of the Church.

1 Kings 7:22
Mark 13:34

1 Cor. 12:4
1 Cor. 7:7

There are "diversities of gifts," but none are without any. "*Every* man hath his proper gift of God, one after this manner, and another after that." If we think it humble to profess, or are humble enough really to believe, that we have but the "one talent," that is the more reason why we should eagerly make the *very* most of it for our Lord; for if it is only one, it is not our own, but our "Lord's money."

Matt. 25:15; Luke 19:16, 20, 23
1 Chron. 29:14

TWENTY-NINTH DAY.

What the Will of the Lord Is.

"Wherefore be ye not unwise, but understanding what the will of the Lord is."
—Ephesians 5:17.

Isaiah 55:8

Matthew 6:10

Ephesians 1:9

Colossians 1:9,10

Ephesians 1:5

2 Cor. 6:18
Ephesians 5:1

Galatians 1:4
Hebrews 10:9
Titus 2:14

2 Cor. 1:10

Hebrews 10:10
2 Thess. 1:11
Hebrews 12:10

ARE we not apt to connect the thoughts of God's will with efforts to submit to what is not very pleasant to us? Is this *fair*, when all that He Himself tells us of His will should make us love and admire and rejoice in it? Truly our thoughts are not His thoughts about it, or there would not be so many a sigh over that glorious petition, " Thy will be done."

Let us see what He says it is, for He hath " made known unto us the mystery of His will "; and in proportion as we are filled with the knowledge of it, shall we walk worthy of the Lord unto all pleasing.

1. It was the good pleasure of His will to predestinate us unto the adoption of children, that we should be His own "sons and daughters," His own " dear children." And if He had told us no more than this, ought not " Thy will be done" to peal forth as an "Amen chorus" from all His adopted ones?

2. It was the will of God our Father that the Lord Jesus Christ should give Himself for our sins, " that He might deliver us from this present evil world." Jesus said, " Lo, I come to do Thy will, O God," and " gave Himself for us, that He might redeem us from all iniquity." And day by day He is delivering those who believe that He " doth deliver," and " trust that He will yet deliver "; for *this* is " the will of the Lord."

3. By this will we are sanctified. Sanctification is the continual fulfilling of the good pleasure of His goodness in us. It is the making us partakers of His holiness and of the

2 Peter 1:4; Rom.
8:29; 2 Cor. 4:11
Matthew 5:6
1 Thess. 4:3
1 Thess. 5:18
Ephesians 5:20
Psalm 71:6, 8, 14,
15

John 3:16
2 Cor. 9:15
Isaiah 45:17;
35:10; 60:19
John 6:40

John 10:28
Titus 1:2; Jn. 6:39
Amos 9:9

John 17:22

John 17:24

1 Thess. 4:17
Psalm 18:44

Psalm 68:19

Luke 2:14
Romans 12:2

divine nature itself. It is making us like Jesus, so that the life of Jesus may be manifest even in our mortal flesh. It is granting the desire, the thirst of thirsts, of every renewed heart. And "*this* is the will of God, even your sanctification!"

4. It is the will of God in Christ Jesus concerning us, that in everything we should give thanks, "always for all things." This implies a life full of cause for praise, and full of power to praise;—can any one describe a brighter ideal? Yet *this* is the will of God concerning *you*.

5. Perishing, failing, dying,—how the very words "everlasting life" shine out to us in the darkness! a resplendent gift purchased for us by the one transcendent gift of God! It includes everlasting salvation, light, joy, love, glory; and it is for *every one* "which seeth the Son and believeth on Him:" for Jesus says, "*This* is the will of Him that sent Me."

6. Is not this enough? is there yet a misgiving and a haunting fear lest we should lose this great gift? Again the glorious will of God is our security; for, though our numb hand might let it slip, we are ourselves in the grasp of a Hand which holds us and our eternal life too; for, of all which the Father hath given Him, He "shall lose nothing," "not the least grain shall fall upon the earth," not you, not I: for "*this* is the Father's will."

7. Now for the climax; and this time it is the Son, our own Lord Jesus Christ, who tells His Father that He is one with Him, and then, in His own divine name, declares His divine will: "I *will* that they also whom Thou hast given Me, be with Me where I am." *This* is the consummation of His will concerning us, that we should be for ever with the Lord! Shall we like "strangers" "submit to this"? Shall we "bow" to this? Shall we dare to *sigh* over "Thy will be done"? Shall we not rather "submit ourselves wholly to His holy will and pleasure," bow under the very load of the benefits of His will in deepest adoration and intensest thanksgiving, and *not* wait for the "happier shore," but here and now *sing* out of the abundance of a simply believing heart, "Thy will be done"? For truly it is "*good* will to men"; and may we be so "transformed by the renewing of our minds,"

that we may daily and joyfully " prove what is that good, and acceptable, and perfect will of God."

With quivering heart and trembling will
    The word hath passed thy lips,
Within the shadow, cold and still,
    Of some fair joy's eclipse.
"Thy will be done!" Thy God hath heard,
And He will crown that faith-framed word.

Thy prayer shall be fulfilled, — but how?
    His thoughts are not as thine;
While thou wouldst only weep and bow,
    He saith, "Arise and shine!"
Thy thoughts were all of grief and night,
But His of boundless joy and light.

Thy Father reigns supreme above;
    The glory of His name
Is Grace and Wisdom, Truth and Love,
    His will must be the same.
And thou hast asked all joys in one,
In whispering forth, "Thy will be done!"

THIRTIETH DAY.

His Last Commandment.

"This do in remembrance of Me."—Luke 22:19.

Psalm 119:19
John 6:63

HIS last commandment! Do we not desire to obey it in its very fullest meaning, to do exactly *what* He meant us to do, and *all* that He meant us to do in it? Let us pray that He may open our eyes to behold wondrous things in it, and enable us to rise through the letter to the spirit.

2 Peter 1:15
Philippians 3:8

It is not simply, "This *do*." We may obey so far month by month or week by week, and yet never once have obeyed our Lord's dying wish or fulfilled His desire. He said, "This do *in remembrance* of Me." We cannot remember what we do not know. We must know the Lord Jesus Christ before we can truly remember Him at His table; for He does not say that we are to do it in remembrance of what He said, or even of what He did. That is quite a different thing. We may remember what we have heard or read of Ridley and Latimer, and we might commemorate their martyrdom; but we cannot remember them, because we never knew them,

2 Cor. 5:16
1 John 2:3
2 Peter 3:18
John 17:3
Proverbs 14:10

except as matter of history. But we know the Lord Jesus Christ as we know no man after the flesh. "We do know that we know Him," and "the knowledge of our Lord and Saviour Jesus Christ" is our very life; it is the joy with which no stranger intermeddleth.

Philippians 3:10
Song. 1:4
John 14:26; 16:4

Without this personal knowledge of Him, there can be no true remembrance of Him in the Lord's Supper. Let us seek to "know Him," so that we may be able to remember Him; then the sweet remembrance of Himself and His exceeding great love will include remembrance of the words and ways of the Lord Jesus; then it will arouse our love into a vivid reality of personal affection; then He will draw nigh

Lament. 3:57
Isaiah 64:5

to us: for "Thou meetest him that rejoiceth and worketh righteousness, those that remember Thee in Thy ways."

Psalm 119:32

Isaiah 26:8

Mk. 14:17; Matt.
26:20; Luke 22:11

Matthew 9:15
Job 37:21
Acts 1:11
Matthew 28:20
Hebrews 13:8
John 17:20
1 Cor. 11:23
Mark 15:30

Song. 2:3
1 Cor. 11:26

Have we not sometimes gone rather to get something for ourselves than simply to remember Him? and may not this account for some of the disappointment, which is no uncommon experience, that we did not run *exactly* in the way of His commandment? We went to get strengthening and refreshing. We went perhaps vaguely expecting some peculiar manifestation of Himself, some almost sensible consciousness of His presence which is quite outside of His written promise or command. We went expecting something *because* we went, a sort of reward in and for the outward act. We remembered our weakness, and our wants, and our wishes, and we forgot that He commanded "one thing"—the remembrance of *Himself.* Shall we not ask the Holy Spirit next time to fix our hearts, so that the whole desire of our soul may be "to Thy name, and to the remembrance of Thee"?

There was no "remembrance" in that first celebration of the Lord's Supper, that first solemn evening communion; for He was bodily present as the Master of the feast. The very word was a shadow cast before of the time when He should "be taken from them." But now "the bright light which was in the cloud" shines all along the dim waiting time, revealing "this same Jesus"; for He whom we specially "remember" at His table, is with us "alway," all the days, "the same yesterday, to-day, and for ever." He loves us now as He loved us when He prayed for "*all* them which shall believe on Me" in "the same night in which He was betrayed." He loves us now as He loved us when He would not come down from the cross to save Himself.

Love is the link between the remembrance and the anticipation; for the two melt into each other, and form one hallowed radiance of present great delight. "For as often as ye eat this bread, and drink this cup, ye do shew the Lord's death *till He come.*" So perhaps some will be showing it forth at the very moment when He comes! What a transition of unimaginable blessedness! It is almost too dazzlingly beautiful to think of.

Luther said: "I feel as if Jesus Christ died yesterday." So fresh, so vivid, be our love and thankfulness! But may we

Psalm 145:7
Titus 2:13, 14

add: "And as if He were coming to-day!" Then our lives would indeed be rich in remembrance and radiant in anticipation, "looking for that blessed hope, and the glorious appearing of the great God and our Saviour Jesus Christ; who gave Himself for us, that He might redeem us from all iniquity."

> According to Thy gracious word,
>   In deep humility,
> This will I do, my gracious Lord,
>   I will remember Thee.
>
> Remember Thee, and all Thy pains,
>   And all Thy love to me;
> Yes, while a breath, a pulse remains,
>   Will I remember Thee.

JAMES MONTGOMERY.

THIRTY-FIRST DAY.

The Great Reward.

"In keeping of them there is great reward."—Psalm 19:11.

Deut. 5:29

NOT, "Because I keep them I shall have a great reward"; but, "*In* keeping of them there *is* great reward." God Himself wants us to keep them, because He loves us. He says: "O that there were such an heart in them, that they would fear Me, and keep *all My commandments always,* that it might be well with them!" This reward is an indisputable, though too often not fully recognised, fact of every Christian's experience. That we may have to keep His commandments in the very teeth of trial, loss, opposition, or distress does not touch the matter; for, nevertheless, not afterward, but *in* the keeping of His words, He takes care to keep His word that there shall be great reward.

Matthew 19:29

John 14:24
Ex. 20:6; Deut. 11:1; John 14:15, etc.

John 3:33

Hebrews 8:10
Romans 5:5

Deut. 5:27
1 John 5:3
Deut. 6:24

If there is not great reward, it only shows that there is not real keeping. The essence of true keeping of God's commandments is love. (See how many times keep and love are joined together in all parts of His word.) Now, if we have only been obeying in mere form and letter, because we were afraid to disobey, this is *not* the heart-obedience which is always crowned with blessings. So, if we cannot quite set to our seal that God is true to this promise, let us be quite sure that it is because we have not fulfilled His condition. And let us now, at once, ask Him to write His laws in our hearts, and so to shed abroad His love in us by the Holy Ghost, that we may begin at once to keep them for very love to our glorious Lawgiver and Mediator. Then we shall know for ourselves that they are not grievous, but that they are "for our good, *always.*"

Yet surely we may appeal to the experience of every one of the King's servants, that, however feeble and imperfect our obedience has been, we do know something about "great reward," not *for* it, but *in* it. As in the days of Hezekiah, when the hand of God was to give them one heart to do the commandment of the king, the result was great gladness, great joy, great blessing, and great prosperity, so is it now in the spiritual reign of our King. Not outward and visible reward, though even that He very often adds, far more exceeding; but inward and spiritual reward.

Not in general only, but in minutest particulars. Having pledged Himself to this, He is "not unrighteous to forget" the least act of Spirit-wrought obedience. Sometimes He puts such wonderful sweetness into the doing of or the refraining from some little thing for His sake, that we wonder what makes us so happy about it, and cannot but be conscious that it is not exactly one's mere natural feeling. Is not this a precious experience of "great reward," all the greater because it came through some very little thing?

Let us put together into a bright bit of Bible-mosaic the scattered gems which are part of this great present reward, "the promise of the life that now is," the hundred-fold which we are to receive "now in *this* time":—1. *Strength:* "Therefore shall ye keep all the commandments ... that ye may be strong"; for "the way of the Lord is strength to the upright." 2. *Safety:* "Whoso keepeth the commandment shall feel no evil thing," much less be hurt by it! 3. *Liberty:* "I will walk at liberty: *for* I seek Thy precepts." Every commandment kept is a fetter of Satan broken by the grace and might of the "stronger than he." 4. *Peace:* "Great peace have they that love Thy law." And in proportion as we hearken to His commandments, does our peace flow as a river. Disobedience dries it all up instantly. 5. *Life and Health:* Perhaps more literally than we suppose; for it stands to reason there is less friction and wear and tear even of our nerves and physique when we keep His peace-bearing commands to trust and not be afraid, to be without carefulness and anxious thought. "Let thine heart keep My commandments: for length of days, and long life, and peace, shall they add to thee." "It is your life." "It shall be health." "I know that His commandment is life everlasting." 6. *Knowledge:* "If

John 7:17	any man will do His will, he shall know of the doctrine."
John 8:31, 32	"If ye continue in My word, ... ye shall know the truth." 7.
1 John 3:22	*Answered Prayers:* "Whatsoever we ask, we receive of Him,
Nehemiah 8:14, 17, etc.	because we keep His commandments." 8. *Gladness:* Again and again we find this the result of seeking out and keep-
John 14:21	ing the commands of God. 9. *The Father's Love:* "He that hath My commandments, and keepeth them, he it is that loveth Me: and he that loveth Me shall be loved of My Fa- ther." 10. *The Manifestation of Jesus:* "And I will love him, and will manifest Myself unto him." 11. *The indwelling of*
John 14:23	*the Triune God:* "And we will come unto him, and make our abode with him." 12. *The Witness of the Spirit to this in-*
1 John 3:24	*dwelling:* "He that keepeth His commandments dwelleth in Him, and He in him. And hereby we know that He abideth in us, by the Spirit which He hath given us."
Hebrews 11:32	"What shall I more say?" *Verily,* in keeping of them there *is* great reward!

"Blessed is the man that feareth the Lord, that delighteth greatly in His commandments."—*Psalm 112:1.*

Note: "The Great Reward" for the "Thirty-First Day" was the last item in *Royal Commandments.* Because extra pages are available in this new edition, these fur- ther items (not published in *Royal Commandments*) are added here at the end: two music scores and two poems by Frances Ridley Havergal.

STAY AND THINK.

Words and Music by
Frances Ridley Havergal

1. Know-ing that the God on high, With a ten - der Fa - ther's grace, Waits to hear your faint - est cry, Waits to show a Fa - ther's face:— Stay and Think! Stay and Think! Stay and Think! Stay and Think! How He loves!— Oh, should not— you Love this— gra - cious Fa - ther too?

2. Knowing Christ was crucified,
    Knowing that He loves you now
Just as much as when He died
    With the thorns upon His brow,—
    Stay and think!—
How He loves! oh, should not you
Love this blessèd Saviour too?

3. Knowing that a Spirit strives
    With your weary, wandering heart,
Who can change the restless lives,
    Pure and perfect peace impart,—
    Stay and think!—
How He loves! oh, should not you
Love this loving Spirit too?

'I Did This for Thee! What Hast Thou Done for Me?'

(MOTTO PLACED UNDER A PICTURE OF OUR SAVIOUR IN THE STUDY OF A GERMAN DIVINE.)

I GAVE My life for thee,	Galatians 2:20.
My precious blood I shed,	1 Peter 1:19.
That thou might'st ransomed be,	Ephesians 1:7.
And quickened from the dead.	Ephesians 2:1.
I gave My life for thee;	Titus 2:14.
What hast thou given for Me?	John 21:15–17.
I spent long years for thee	1 Timothy 1:15.
In weariness and woe,	Isaiah 53:3.
That an eternity	John 17:24.
Of joy thou mightest know.	John 16:22.
I spent long years for thee;	John 1:10, 11.
Hast thou spent *one* for Me?	1 Peter 4:2.
My Father's home of light,	John 17:5.
My rainbow-circled throne,	Revelation 4:3.
I left, for earthly night,	Philippians 2:7.
For wanderings sad and lone.	Matthew 8:20.
I left it all for thee;	2 Corinthians 8:9.
Hast thou left aught for Me?	Luke 10:29.
I suffered much for thee,	Isaiah 53:5.
More than thy tongue may tell,	Matthew 26:39.
Of bitterest agony,	Luke 22:44.
To rescue thee from hell.	Romans 5:9.
I suffered much for thee;	1 Peter 2:21–24.
What canst thou bear for Me?	Romans 8:17, 18.
And I have brought to thee,	John 4:10, 14.
Down from My home above,	John 3:13.
Salvation full and free,	Revelation 21:6.
My pardon and My love.	Acts 5:31.
Great gifts I brought to thee;	Psalm 68:18.
What hast thou brought to Me?	Romans 12:1.

Oh, let thy life be given,	Romans 6:13.
Thy years for Him be spent,	2 Corinthians 5:15.
World-fetters all be riven,	Philippians 3:8.
And joy with suffering blent;	1 Peter 4:13–16.
I gave Myself for thee:	Ephesians 5:2.
Give thou *thyself* to Me!	Proverbs 23:26.

Frances Ridley Havergal

Jesus, I will trust Thee.

Jesus, I will trust Thee, trust Thee with my soul;
Guilty, lost, and helpless, Thou canst make me whole.
There is none in heaven or on earth like Thee,
Thou hast died for sinners, therefore, Lord, for me.

Jesus, I may trust Thee, name of matchless worth!
Spoken by the angel at Thy wondrous birth;
Written, and for ever, on Thy cross of shame,
Sinners read, and worship, trusting in that name.

Jesus, I must trust Thee, pondering Thy ways:
Full of love and mercy, all Thine earthly days,
Sinners gathered round Thee, lepers sought Thy face,—
None too vile or loathsome for a Saviour's grace.

Jesus, I can trust Thee, trust Thy written word,
Though Thy voice of pity I have never heard.
When Thy Spirit teacheth, to my taste how sweet!
Only may I hearken, sitting at Thy feet!

Jesus, I do trust Thee, trust without a doubt,
Whosoever cometh, Thou wilt not cast out!
Faithful is Thy promise, precious is Thy blood—
These my soul's salvation, Thou my Saviour-God!

Mary Jane (Deck) Walker

Jesus, I will trust Thee.

Words by Mary Jane (Deck) Walker
Music by Frances Ridley Havergal

1. Je - sus, I will trust Thee, trust Thee with my soul;

Guil - ty, lost, and help - less, Thou canst make me whole.

There is none in hea - ven or on earth like Thee.

Thou hast died for sin - ners, there-fore, Lord, for me. A - men.

To Thee.

'Lord, to whom shall we go?'—JOHN 6:68.

I BRING my sins to Thee,
    The sins I cannot count,
That all may cleansèd be
    In Thy once opened Fount.
I bring them, Saviour, all to Thee,
The burden is too great for me.

My heart to Thee I bring,
    The heart I cannot read;
A faithless, wandering thing,
    An evil heart indeed.
I bring it, Saviour, now to Thee,
That fixed and faithful it may be.

To Thee I bring my care,
    The care I cannot flee;
Thou wilt not only share,
    But bear it all for me.
O loving Saviour, now to Thee
I bring the load that wearies me.

I bring my grief to Thee,
    The grief I cannot tell;
No words shall needed be,
    Thou knowest all so well.
I bring the sorrow laid on me,
O suffering Saviour, now to Thee.

My joys to Thee I bring,
    The joys Thy love hath given,
That each may be a wing
    To lift me nearer heaven.
I bring them, Saviour, all to Thee,
For Thou hast purchased all for me.

My life I bring to Thee,
    I would not be my own;
O Saviour, let me be
    Thine ever, Thine alone.
My heart, my life, my all I bring
To Thee, my Saviour and my King!

F.R.H.

www.ingramcontent.com/pod-product-compliance
Lightning Source LLC
Chambersburg PA
CBHW070541030426
42337CB00016B/2297